FIND YOUR "SELF-CULTURE"

Moving from Depression and Anxiety to Monumental Self-Acceptance

Victoria Lorient-Faibish, MEd, CCC, BCPP, RPE
Holistic Psychotherapist, Life Coach and Speaker

MASSenergy Press

Cataloguing data available from Library and Archives Canada.

Softcover: ISBN 978-0-9921237-0-3
Ebook – Kindle: ISBN 978-0-9921237-1-0
Ebook – epub: ISBN 978-0-9921237-2-7

Published by: MASSenergy Press, info@visualizationworks.com

Design and layout by Beth Crane, WeMakeBooks
Cover design by Cindy Cake, WeMakeBooks
Author photograph by Ricco Tiburzi
Illustrations by Homa Bahadouri
Edited by Andrea Lemieux
Index by Judith Brand

Author's note: The case studies in this book are amalgams of several people and do not pertain to any one person. In addition, all names are fictitious, and other features, such as sex and occupation, have been changed to protect the subjects' identities.

Printed and bound in Canada

"Everything is energy and that's all there is to it.
Match the frequency of the reality you want and you
cannot help but get that reality. It can be no other way.
This is not philosophy. This is physics."
— Albert Einstein

CONTENTS

Introduction

I have been a holistic psychotherapist for over twenty-two years. I often joked that I might as well have had a machete in my hand as I carved a previously unchartered path in my career and in my city. The holistic way was not at all mainstream in Toronto in 1990. But deep in my soul, I knew this was the way for me. To follow the mainstream path would have been to betray my very instincts. I could not lie to myself; my being would not have tolerated that.

I did study and get a master's degree to assuage the part of me that needed to feel I had some academic support from the mainstream, and at the same time, I felt that it honored the side of me that loves to learn and to grow. I also spent eight years studying Eastern body-centered healing modalities, including my beloved polarity therapy,[1] which I fondly call the "Rolls Royce of bodywork." I am also a reiki[2] master, and I use visualization, focusing

---

1 Polarity therapy was created by Dr. Randolph Stone, DO, DC, ND (1890–1981), an American osteopath born in Austria. This therapy blends Western medicine and the wisdom of Eastern traditions in a holistic, energy-based system that works on the whole body to balance the subtle and natural electromagnetic energy that makes up our physical, mental, emotional and spiritual selves to enhance overall health and well-being. Polarity therapy addresses life and health issues through hands-on bodywork, nutrition, exercise and communication.

2 Reiki was developed by Japanese Buddhist Mikao Usui in 1922. The term *reiki* comes from the Japanese word *rei*, which means "universal," and *ki*, which means "vital life-force energy," which flows through all living things. Reiki practitioners use a hands-on approach to transfer universal energy for healing on a physical, mental, emotional and spiritual level.

and craniosacral therapy[3] in the psychotherapy work that I offer.

Over the past twenty-plus years, I have learned that talking alone does not work in transforming a mind and its emotions, or a life. I asked myself why people continue for years to undergo psychoanalysis or psychotherapy when nothing changes. What is missing? In my opinion, it is the multidimensional and multisensorial way of addressing the various emotional blockages that people may have. They may talk and talk about how they do not feel fulfilled or able to be their authentic selves, but nothing can change without creating new belief systems. In my practice, I help people find their true power through a multilayered approach, not just through the mind, but the body and spirit as well. It is not about throwing away what is there already, but adding to it.

Almost every person with anxiety or depression who walks into my office benefits from going through a process of learning who they really are—that is, identifying the motivations, patterns, thoughts and experiences that they are living. Through this process, they are able to see lucidly what has prevented them from finding their *self-culture*, and thus they are able to bring forth their authentic voice and self-empowerment. The concept of self-culture is not complicated, and, in my opinion, it is infinitely necessary to experience true joy in life. I believe that we were put on the planet to experience joy and fulfillment ourselves—and then to give to others. From here we can affect the planet in positive ways.

3 Craniosacral therapy was pioneered by osteopathic physician Dr. John E. Upledger after years of clinical testing and research at Michigan State University. This therapy is a gentle, hands-on approach that releases stress deep in the body to relieve pain and dysfunction and improve whole-body health.

I feel so blessed to live in a time and place that does not condemn me for being myself, while I forge a path that is all my own. In the past, so many were tortured, imprisoned, maligned, shut down, rejected and ostracized for daring to be original, authentic, unique, empowered and vocal. In some parts of the planet, this is still happening. I feel deeply in my heart for those who are suffering right now for speaking their truth and for being themselves. May we all support those who are on the path to selfhood. May all those who suffer due to a quest to be authentic be protected and freed from any prison they are in, even if it is a prison of their own making.

Through this book, I hope to bring the transformational work that I do in my office to a wider audience. One of the key laws of the universe is the Law of Attraction, in which like attracts like. I see this law in action in my life every day; for example, the clients who walk through my door are those who are attracted to my holistic approach and are ready for change and to step into their greatness. Similarly, if you have been drawn to read this book, you are ready to embrace the vibration of transformation. In this book you will find many tools to work with, and, if you choose to use them consistently, the change you seek will occur. You will find the validation that will encourage you to begin your quest to find and be yourself, and to embrace your uniqueness: your *self-culture*!

Chapter One

Finding Your "Self-Culture"

If you have not yet found your *self-culture*—your authentic, instinctive self—you are not living the life the universe intends for you. The planet needs the real you, and it is time that you began the journey! The pursuit of self-culture is a hard one for many of us, and I have unlimited compassion for those who embark on this path.

What is your inner voice saying? What makes your heart happy? What brings you joy? Who is your real self? What path are you on? And what do you want out of your life? You need to know the answers to these questions to live your life in the best way you can. The quest for your self-culture is not a narcissistic, futile, self-indulgent pursuit. It is vital to your well-being. You can serve those you love and the planet better when you know who you are and are at peace with yourself. This peace does not come without the "spiritual warrior" part of you doing its finest battle on your behalf. The journey is a profound, and at times arduous, look within. The result will be an emerging self that you will treasure, savor and protect because you know you fought for it and won!

Whatever ails you, whether it be depression, anxiety, addiction, unhappiness, relationship issues or any other emotional disharmony, finding your self-culture is key to healing. There is no doubt that brain chemistry, nutrition, spirituality, support, cognitive changes and discipline are part of the recipe for success in the reversal of chronic mental disharmony, but the journey to find and live your self-culture is essential to being a balanced adult.

There is no way around the mountain; you must go through it on all levels: body, mind and spirit. There will be pain and discomfort when defining your own "culture" in the face of the strong and imposing cultures of your society and family and their long-held belief systems. This does not at all mean total amputation of your *family culture* or society. But you will need a period of adjustment for your new normal to surface and stick. The joy you derive from living your own self-cultural truth will be matched, to be sure, by the conflict that can ensue during the process. But the thing to hold onto at every turn is the fact that you, and only you, are the one living your life. No one else is. True joy comes from unearthing your true self from the depths of your soul.

Self-Culture versus Family Culture

Before we can define *self-culture*, we need to look at what *culture* is. Anthropologist Edward Burnett Tylor wrote that culture is "that complex whole which includes knowledge, belief, art, morals, law, custom, and any other capabilities and habits acquired by man as a member of society."[1] Culture is the full range of learned human behavior patterns, such as ritual, habits and customs. Culture is a powerful tool for survival, but it is a fragile phenomenon, constantly changing and easily lost because it exists only in our minds.

Your family culture is all you know in the beginning. It influences all aspects of your life. This is something you engage in without thinking. It is something that gives you a sense of community, belonging and family—when it is working for you. When it is not, it may cause you to feel unhappy. It can exert undue pressure on

1 Edward Burnett Tylor, *Primitive Culture: Researches into the Development of Mythology, Philosophy, Religion, Art, and Custom*, Vol. 1 (London: John Murray, 1871), 1.

you to conform and fit into what your family knows and has done for generations. To define yourself, or your self-culture, in the midst of this pressure is very difficult, and if you find you are not able to be free to be yourself, a feeling of unhappiness can permeate your life. Even if you are happy within the construct of your family culture, the journey to knowing yourself better and defining who you are is a worthy endeavor. Finding one's self-culture is valuable for all who walk the planet, especially for those who feel like aliens in their own homes.

When we do not look inside to hear the voice that is truly our own, we are actually living an amalgam of our family culture and our societal culture rather unconsciously. This can either work for us or betray us. If it is betraying us, we can become depressed and anxious. I have seen deeply unhappy people who appear to be happy on the outside, but inside, in the quiet of their lives, that happiness is not there. It is a facade that is masking deep unhappiness. Through the case studies and exercises in this book, you can work to unearth your true self-culture, which is lying in your subconscious or unconscious, and with new realizations and awareness, uncover the authentic you that is longing to get out.

Total self-sacrifice in favor of the well-being of your family culture will not lead you to feelings of joy. Instead, it will result in depression, resentment and eventual embitterment. It is important to be true to yourself as a means to create joy. You need to fill your own cup first and give to others from the overflow. When I refer to your family culture, I do not mean your country of origin or religion, although these do play a part. Family culture is the emotional baggage handed down through generations that profoundly affects the life of any given family. The relationships, such as between parents and children, brothers and sisters, grandparents and grandchildren, are the real meat of the issue, and from where a family culture derives. These relationships influence how a person turns out. If individual needs and wants are constantly subjugated in favor of the group, that person's well-being will be negatively affected, or if the emotional needs of all in the family are silenced in the face of one overbearing family member, things will turn out badly for those who have learned to silence their own authenticity just to survive this type of family minefield.

I see many people who are not living authentically and, therefore, are suffering terribly. They are struggling within, wanting to be who they truly are, yet having to contend with their beloved family, who puts so much pressure on them to conform with the family culture. They mistakenly believe that guilt can be avoided by obeying the rules and not disappointing or displeasing the family. But this leads to self-sabotage, which is profoundly self-destructive.

It is important to remember that uncovering your true self brings with it responsibility as well. This quest is not permission to wage a full-scale rebellion against your parental culture. That would indicate that you are coming from your hurt child/teenage self, who feels the need to revolt in order to establish boundaries and preferences. Instead, when you are coming from your adult self, you know that you do not need to be aggressive or arrogant in your bid for selfhood. You accept it as fact that you must act in peaceful, nondefensive ways to establish the new normal of your own self-culture. In addition, I advise that you do your own inner work before announcing your plans to anyone. I firmly believe that doing versus telling is the best way to engage in new ways of behaving.

Most parents and loved ones truly want what is best for their children and relatives, so trust that your journey will eventually be accepted by the old guard. Be mindful that finding and living your self-culture may not occur very quickly or very easily. But time has a way of doing its healing work. Soon, with practice and diligence, you will be living the life of your choosing, in which you are on the top of your own priority list, and your family is still a blessed part of your life—but not the main show. This balancing act is necessary for your development as a reasonable and balanced adult who is facing the world on your own terms.

Getting to Work

So grab your shovels! You will be digging—excavating into the self—and at the same time creating a little necessary perturbation as you begin your journey to self-culture. It is profoundly important to do some deep emotional mining. You need to see if you are feeling any resentment about your present situation. Ask yourself these questions: Do I feel deprived of my authentic truth while living within my family culture, my job, my community, my marriage or my society at large? Am I giving all of myself to others and leaving very little for myself? Have I been ignoring my true feelings about the state of my life? Am I living my life in my own way, or as someone else's version of what is best for me?

If you answered yes to some or all of these questions, then you have some work to do. No one else is going to save you. *You* have to do the work of finding your self-culture. You, and you alone, are responsible for your life. You cannot blame others for your life situation; you have to do the work to have the life you want for yourself.

As you seek your authentic self, you may feel guilty for defining your own self-culture and establishing your empowered voice. We will tackle this in various sections in this book so that you can conquer your feelings of guilt. But the first thing you have to do to overcome guilt is to give yourself permission to be different from your family. Tell yourself that it is healthy and normal to establish your own way of being and distinguish yourself from others; that is, to "individuate." Many spiritual texts also expound on the benefits of being true to oneself.

Another way to help you alleviate your guilt is to establish what you are reasonably able to commit to regarding your dedication to your family and its culture. Be brutally honest with yourself. If you give more than you truly want to, resentment will creep in once again. Similarly, if you don't give anything at all, guilt will do its damage. Thus, the course of your journey is a dance between guilt and self-culture that you will need to analyze often and honestly.

Chapter Two

BEGINNING THE JOURNEY

Selfy versus Selfish

I like the made-up word "selfy" instead of "selfish," which means being concerned only with advantages for oneself without regard for others. You may feel that pursuing your self-culture will make you appear to be mean, selfish and unkind. Yes, the journey does involve *you*; however, you cannot help others unless you are filled with vitality yourself, and so I encourage an attitude of "selfyness." Selfyness involves the consistent act of listening deeply to your true inner voice and allowing it to be louder than all other voices or opinions. It is personalized self-care. Unless you focus on yourself first, your attempts to give to others from an empty vessel will inevitably result in burnout.

Trouble sleeping, digestive problems, feeling anxious or depressed or experiencing any other imbalance are examples of your body's way of trying to tell you something. It is asking if you are listening to yourself and your needs. If you are not paying attention, your body will speak to you more loudly by increasing your symptoms. Lack of awareness, or selfyness, can also drive a person to seek validation through external means, which may show up as addictions and compulsive behavior that make the person feel vital, but only numb their pain. It is a false vitality.

The Spiritual Warrior

Finding your self-culture is hero's work. I liken it to the journey of a warrior who is preparing for battle. There is no violence in this battle, but there is a plan of attack and a methodology that you need to employ to complete the journey. There are many forces out there that can dissuade you from being who you truly are. But no permanent change can occur without discipline, commitment and diligence, and because we tend to learn more profoundly through pain, I wish you the gift of despair! This may sound cruel, but pain is the great motivator, and people tend to be more teachable when they are in despair.

When people come into my office feeling despair, anxiety or depression, we engage in therapy designed to uncover the triggers to their unhappiness. We look at the messaging they have ingested and metabolized as truth but that now, as adults, just does not feel authentic. Because of conditioning, they feel trapped by the disease-to-please, obligation, stress, expenses they cannot afford and judgment from others. They come to me to see if there is a way out of their misery—and there is! But the journey requires the strength of a spiritual warrior.

There is no way around the mountain of pain and darkness; you have to go through it to get to the light on the other side. I see this part of the journey to selfhood as a crusade in which you need to pull out all the tools to support you on the sometimes arduous trek. Part of being a spiritual warrior is having the courage to shine a light on the monsters that are keeping you stuck—to look at the obstacles to finding your self-culture squarely in the eye—and when you see the dark within, you have to *name it*, *claim it* and then *transform it*. The toxic patterns, the feelings of turmoil, the dysfunctional relationships are all part of the darkness. The only way to neutralize and transform any part of yourself that is causing you pain and grief is to completely and courageously shine a light on it. In this way, you will be able to truly understand yourself and the motives that keep you down. You will be able to bring the monster out of the unconscious realm. You cannot change the monster or learn from it if you are not aware of it. Also, you cannot learn from the dark parts of yourself if you judge these parts. Drawing on the strength of your spiritual warrior to look at these darker aspects from a more neutral stance will help to put you in a space where you are teachable. You will be less reactive and, therefore, more receptive to understanding any spiritual lessons that your buried monster, if released, could teach you.

The Benefits of Holistic Psychotherapy

My style of holistic psychotherapy, which involves bodywork and visualization, as well as talk, is a powerful and extremely effective way to tap into the messages that the body is trying to express and bring to the fore.

Body-centered therapy addresses memory at the cellular level of a trauma or other event that a person may have experienced. Therapies such as craniosacral, reiki, myofascial and my favorite, polarity therapy, stimulate the relaxation response of the parasympathetic nervous system. As such, the client is then able to move through painful, stressful therapy and still maintain a sense of ease and relaxation.

In my practice, I have had clients come to me who have often spent years in traditional talk therapy, and yet nothing has changed; they feel the same as they did when they began. When they engage in this form of holistic psychotherapy, they begin to change very quickly. Their behavior shifts and their perspective changes as well. I feel traditional talk therapy keeps people stuck because they tend to get lost in the content of their stories, and, as a result, their negative states of being and the neural pathways associated with their long-held beliefs are reinforced. If all they do is talk and complain, the shame, anger, guilt and victimhood is the main focus and tends to drive the story deeper into their consciousness. More is needed for a shift to happen. Bodywork slows everything down. It makes the therapy content easier to digest. The emotions associated with traumatic and other negative events tend to repeat themselves in our minds and bodies until we are able to fully resolve them. Bodywork and visualization, along with psychotherapeutic exploration, can profoundly stop these repetitive patterns.

This combination helps the client to process the traumatic event that brings out the pain, fear and anxiety from the past to the surface, yet assists the person to stay calm. Visualization exercises encourage self-realization and help a person feel empowered to make changes in their lives. Since the brain doesn't differentiate between the real and the imagined in the way it reacts biochemically, new neural pathways are developed, thus allowing perspectives to change and behaviors to shift.

Bodywork alone, without cognitive awareness, does not allow the information to be fully processed, and talking on its own does not go deeply enough into the trauma. It is the combination that works in an alchemical way to affect transformation.

"Homeplay"[1] is another aspect of my practice, whereby, following a session, I give my clients exercises to do at home. This reinforces the new insights they learned in the office and engages

1 *Homeplay* is a word I like to use to reframe the concept of "homework." I learned this word in my polarity therapy training from one of my teachers, Sher Smith.

them between sessions in experiencing their new perspectives. As a result, their new way of looking at things becomes their new normal.

Case Study: Talking about Pain

Many people ask me what the purpose is of talking about the past or the pain. They just want to cut that time out of their lives. The truth is, up until they came through my door, that was exactly what they had been trying to do. But it doesn't work. It just drives the pattern or the pain deeper into their subconscious or unconscious, and this, in turn, has a way of causing them to attract more of the same toward them.

Post-traumatic stress disorder (PTSD) is a perfect example of this. PTSD can occur after a person has been traumatized. Very often after a trauma, a person will either not have the safe space to speak about what happened, or they may not even want to speak about it. The fear and the feelings remain frozen in their system. They long to be released, but the releasing will cause pain, so the person goes about the business, either consciously or not, of repressing the memories and feelings associated with the traumatic event. They may feel shame, guilt or rage, but do not express it; instead, these feelings transform into a profound intention to numb it all out. As a result, they develop conditions such as addictions, dissociation from self and codependency—all ways to stop feeling the pain.

This is exemplified by Jane, who refused to look at what drove her to binge drink until she blacked out. This type A person seemed to have it all under control—except that she had become frightened because her episodes of drinking and blacking out were becoming more serious.

In my first session with Jane, I asked her why she was drinking, and she said, "It's the only thing that stops my neck and shoulders from hurting. It's just physical, but my partner wants me to get some therapy, so here I am. But, really, I'm great. I've just got neck and shoulder pain."

She spent most of the session quipping and smiling and telling me how great her life was. As an adrenaline junkie, she did everything to excess. She was adept at ignoring the pain and was proud that she was able to "grin and bear it." "Taking a break is for wimps," she said. "In sales you gotta move fast or be left in the dust." And even though her doctor had told her to slow down her running routine, she had kept doing it because of the high she got from it. However, each time I saw her, she would have a new ailment. First it was her neck and shoulders, then an injured foot, stomach problems and crying while asleep—but she would laugh it all off as if it were trivial. Her life was built around ignoring the messages her body and emotions were sending her.

In our second session, I asked Jane to close her eyes.[2] She hated this, but she obliged. This was the journey into the dark—somatic journeying to the core of her being. With this work, we were able to more efficiently tune into the messages her body was trying to send her. When the body senses that an openness is finally being allowed, the information starts to flow.

---

2 I find that most of the talk-therapy portion of my work is best done with the client's eyes closed. People tend to be guarded when their eyes are open, especially with a new therapist. With their eyes closed, people are less likely to focus on my opinion or facial expression, or to feel the need for my approval. They are better able to shut off external stimulus, focus on their inner journey, reach their subconscious more quickly and find answers deep within their souls.

Bringing the Dark into the Light

As Jane lay comfortably with her eyes closed and a pillow under her knees to ease any back pressure. I covered her eyes with a flaxseed pillow, which is comforting and helps to block out the light, and I asked her to breathe continuously without pauses so that as soon as she got to the top of the inhale, she began to exhale, and when she got to the bottom of the exhale, she began to inhale. I sprayed a solution of lavender and sandalwood in her vicinity to open up her olfactory senses, and I played soothing music to cut out anything that might distract her and to help her to focus on the job at hand—going deep within.

As I began to apply a combination of reiki and polarity therapy to help her relax and unwind, I then asked her to tune into the part of her body that was most painful. She told me that she was focusing on her neck and shoulder area. I asked if there were any emotions associated with this physical pain, but she couldn't connect with the emotions at all. I asked her to imagine slowly sending her breath into the painful area. After a long pause, I observed a slight relaxation in her face, as if the pain were easing a little. I knew then that we were on the right track. I then asked her to mentally dialogue with her neck and shoulder area. She said this would be impossible, so I asked her to imagine that she was in a tiny submarine that was traveling to the core of the cells in her neck and shoulder area. (Please see the "Submarine Exercise" in appendix IX.) After another long pause, I asked her to ask this part of her body to speak to her in any way it could. Slowly, an image appeared before her eyes; she was startled by its clarity, saying that she could never have imagined this happening. I gave her some time, and then I gently asked her to describe the image as best she could. She struggled with this, unsure of what she was seeing. I told her to try to get a "felt sense"[3] of it. Gradually, she was able to describe the image—a distinct memory of herself as a child of four or five years old. There was another long pause as her emotions began to flow and she was able to further describe the image. She saw herself as a young child sitting on the floor in the family kitchen. She was playing alone, and she felt lonely, but she had no one to tell. After another long pause, Jane said that she was no longer connected to the image. She had taken herself out of it. She wanted to know what time it was and if we were almost done. She became fidgety, and then her neck pain began to act up again.

I asked her to slow her breath again and imagine sending it into her neck. (I knew that the pain in her neck was speaking the loudest to her.) As she breathed, the memories began to flood in again. She was connecting to her inner self once more. This time, Jane gained more insight into her constant pain; together we learned that it was related to the trauma, pain and loneliness of a childhood where she wasn't permitted to show her emotions. She told me that she wanted to tell her parents how she felt, but no one in the family was allowed to express their feelings because "we are not allowed to upset your dad. He has enough on his plate." In her family, they "just got on with it." Complaining was not allowed; you just did whatever it took and you didn't talk about your feelings. Her father was a quiet alcoholic who came home and drank and was silent. He occasionally would rage at the kids, during which they were expected to remain silent. Jane said, "We never knew when he would blow, so we always felt as though we were

3 Peter A. Levine, author of *Waking the Tiger: Healing Trauma*, describes "felt sense" as internal body sensations, or physical knowing, that we can tune into for information about something we have experienced but have not yet been able to express in words; for example, an old emotional hurt that manifests as physical pain. By focusing on this felt sense, a person can tune into an awareness of the emotional message behind the pain, from which insights can be derived.

walking on egg shells, feeling tense and stressed for fear of making a mistake." She said that finances were uncertain, and her mom was always worried. In her closed-eyes state, Jane was able to realize that there had been room only for her mom's feelings and her dad's rage. Jane's trauma was not from one incident; it was from years of ingesting the message that her feelings didn't matter and shouldn't be listened to. To cope and fit into her family culture, Jane learned to disconnect from her true feelings, words and needs. All that unexpressed energy was frozen in her body. In order to cope, she had lost touch with herself, and she had created a profound inability to trust and honor her own feelings.

Finding the Resources within to Heal

I asked Jane to visualize herself as an adult entering the kitchen, where, as a child, she was sitting on the floor playing alone. I asked her to sit down on the floor next to her younger self. Jane told me that she could see them playing together; connecting silently. After a long pause, Jane's emotions began to flow as they continued to play together. The pain that Jane was feeling, and that she had always tried to avoid, was the mountain that she had to go through. Through her tears, she said that she felt as if she was rediscovering a lost part of herself for the first time in a very long time. I asked her to slowly and gently speak to her younger self. I told her to ask her younger self how she was feeling as she was playing alone on the kitchen floor. At first, Jane said the child said nothing, only her facial expression changed to one of sadness, and then tears welled up in her eyes. She told me she knew that young Jane was forcing herself not to cry. After another long pause, I asked Jane to gently say to her younger self, "It's okay to feel sad," and then, "It's okay to cry."

After a while, I asked Jane to very slowly reach over and touch young Jane's hand. I coaxed her to tell her younger self that she was there now and that she was sorry they had lost contact for so long and to promise her young self that she was now committed to staying in contact with her. I asked her to say, "You can count on me now." When I asked Jane if she was getting through to her, there was a long pause, and then she finally said yes. A little while later, I asked Jane to gently invite young Jane to sit on her lap. When Jane indicated that young Jane was on her lap, I told her to cradle her as if she were her mother.

With this exercise, a profound connection began to be created between Jane and her younger hurt-child self, and a healing of this part of herself began to occur. The session was winding down, but before we stopped, I asked Jane to take a snapshot in her mind's eye of this image of herself and young Jane in a maternal embrace. I then asked her to imagine placing the image into her heart area so that she could access it at a later date. With this act, a new cellular memory was created that anchored the work that had been done. We would then be able to use this image to access her new insight more easily at a future session.

When I removed the flaxseed pillow from Jane's eyes and turned off the music, Jane said that until then, she had no idea what she had been feeling inside. It had all come as a shock to her. She thought the past was done and gone. And then the realization slowly came to her about the choices she had been making in her life.

As a homeplay exercise, I asked her to write down all that she recalled of the session when she got home. I also asked her to do this after every session as a way to keep a journal of all the discoveries she made. The act of writing it all down further anchors a person's new understanding on a deeper level.

In future sessions, Jane became much more forthcoming with the truth of her emotions. Therapy became a sanctuary for her, and she used it as a real opportunity for transformation. Her quest for self-culture was not what she had set out to do, but it is what happened. She changed her life in very concrete ways, including living more within her means. Her high-octane, adrenaline-filled lifestyle could not be maintained without dire consequences, and she started to make new choices with regards to the pressure she allowed in her life. Before she came to me for therapy, she had always played the role of the solution-finder for the problems of others; her own needs were always low on her priority list, only to come out boldly when she drank. After her therapeutic work, she did a full housecleaning of her relationships and began to insist on having her needs heard and met.

It is important to mention that this kind of transformation is slow and organic. Jane had trouble coping with her pattern of binge drinking; it didn't fall away easily. She also had to do a lot of twelve-step work with Alcoholics Anonymous in addition to her therapy with me.

Working with Yourself

Now that you have read the description of my session with Jane, I encourage you to try a similar journey on your own using the "Deep Relaxation Exercise" in appendix I. Even though you are not receiving bodywork while you do this exercise, you will benefit. You can mimic the effects of the bodywork by making sure you breathe slowly so that you remain relaxed.

After you do some work like this for yourself, please write down all the thoughts, feelings, images and epiphanies you might have. This will help you to retain them at a deeper level, and they will be beneficial to you as a reference to the new discoveries you make at a later date.

Looking at the darkness within has a transformational effect. As you name the truth of it, you can claim or own it. Once you own it, you are no longer at the mercy of it. You will have brought the dark into the light, so it can no longer dominate you. You stop the *Wizard of Oz syndrome*, in which you essentially peel back the curtain and see that it is not a big, overpowering force, but a smaller, more manageable concept that is yours to work with. Therefore, you can work with what you know rather than with something that you are unconscious of. Once you have the awareness, you cannot un-ring that bell. You cannot un-know what you know. It is in the conscious realm now, and that is a place of power; that is the beginning of finding true self-culture.

Challenge Your Old, Concretized Beliefs

It is vital that you challenge your old thoughts and beliefs in order to finally find your self-culture and live by it. These patterns no longer serve you. You need to do this without diminishing or mocking yourself. If you challenge your concretized beliefs, you will succeed in pushing your unconscious thoughts into your conscious mind, where you can best work to transform them.

Sentences that start with "I will never …," "I am always …" or "It is always [this way]" are examples of thoughts that are concretized and need to be challenged. Do you ever find yourself saying any of the following sentences?

- I'm never good enough.
- People always reject me.
- People don't like me.
- I'm never safe with other people.
- I'm never comfortable speaking in public.

- I'm always worried about things.

When you catch yourself making statements like these, begin a dialogue with them. Respond with statements such as, "That's not true. This may be how it used to be, but now I am open to being different. Just because the past was like this doesn't mean the future will be as well."

Ask questions that challenge the validity of your thought or belief; for example, "Are you 100% sure this is true?" The truth is, we can't be 100% sure of anything, especially if the belief or thought is about what you think other people think about you.

Awareness is the key. You need to be aware of your old beliefs, habits and thoughts to be able to catch them. And if you don't catch them and challenge them, they will hang around even while you are moving toward embracing your self-culture. They will scream to be fed in a last-ditch effort to remain alive. You can liken this to trying to come off sugar. When you begin, the sugar cravings can be intense, and it takes discipline to not give into them. Similarly, you need mental discipline to not give into your long-held negativity.

You Cannot Do It Alone!

All of this does require fortitude and a commitment to the process, and you cannot do it alone. When you go down this path, it will often feel as though you are taking many leaps of faith. But know that with every leap, there will be a net to catch you as you fly. The real you will be there to catch you, and so I encourage you to go on the journey, but don't do it alone, especially if you are feeling abandoned by those who are close to you as you individuate. Know that "nature abhors a vacuum"![4] Whatever void you create

4 Translation of the Latin saying *Natura abhorret a vacua*.

through your passage into selfhood, life will fill it, and you must fill it with supportive entities. Therapy is a good place to start to fill a void. I also highly recommend resources such as twelve-step groups. Combining therapy with a twelve-step program is a profound spiritual-warrior combination that will work, and it goes a long way toward supporting and maintaining a person's emotional health. Adult Children of Alcoholics/Dysfunctional Families (ACA) is an amazing organization for those who are not addicted to a substance, but who come from dysfunctional families and have developed addictions to people and toxic emotions. Co-Dependents Anonymous, Al-Anon, Alcoholics Anonymous and Overeaters Anonymous are also fantastic places to feel supported by other people who are on journeys toward self-culture. Therapy is not always enough; there is also a need between sessions to reinforce the therapy. These organizations offer fellowship, and the people you meet may very well be the people who fill the void when you are individuating.

Staying There!

Working toward self-culture and healing from pain and trauma cannot be sustained without constant practice and discipline. Tools such as meditation, visualization, therapy, journaling, service work, nonaddiction-oriented behavior, mentorship relationships, being physically proactive with your health, surrounding yourself with positive like-minded support and prayer are all helpful to stay on the path. Even if you fall off periodically, the more committed you are to "right" relationship with yourself and life, the easier it will be to stay there, and the more likely you will be to find and keep your self-culture.

Chapter Three

UNDERSTANDING CHANGE

Neural Pathways: The Biology of Change

As you begin your journey of transformation, it is helpful to understand the part your brain plays when you try to change beliefs and old patterns of behavior. The brain has thin neural pathways and thick ones; they could be compared to footpaths and highways. Your long-held beliefs and behavior patterns, those that are inherited and learned through your society, family culture and family dynamics, are ingrained in the wide, complex highway networks of your neural pathways, whereas newer beliefs and behavior patterns form in simple, narrow footpaths in your brain. The former are harder to change because, having been there so long, buried in your unconscious, you act without self-awareness according to your long-held beliefs and behavior patterns.

Look at your family dynamic and see what stands out. What is their "normal" everyday way of being—habits that you may never have questioned and just accepted as your family's mode of behavior. Examples are habits such as constantly interrupting; controlling others by making them feel guilty; raging; and feeling negative, anxious, worried or fearful. It can be difficult to change this negative behavior in yourself, but don't beat yourself up if you have not been able to change a pattern; after all, it has been with you since childhood—it is all you knew. However, don't give up either. There are proven ways to tackle this kind of change. You are up against your biology, but you need not be beaten by it! The more you practice a new behavior, the more likely you are to shift it to the more desired pattern you are seeking. Repetition creates highways of the neural pathways, making the new behavior easier to maintain.

In his book *The Brain That Changes Itself: Stories of Personal Triumph from the Frontiers of Brain Science*, Norman Doidge explains that our brains learn to adapt, and the brain's very matrix changes with repetitive, colorful, multisensorial exposure. Your brain will collaborate with you to change if you repeatedly expose it to new opportunities and experiences that are associated with the self-culture you are uncovering.

Visualization

Repetitive meditation and visualization are fundamental techniques for creating new neural pathways and achieving change. In a meditative state, you can visualize yourself living the life you want to live. When you do this, it is important to make your image as clear, colorful and specific as you can. You can also use other methods to express your vision, such as writing it, speaking it, singing it, acting it, drawing it and incorporating movement with your visualization, such as putting your hand to your heart or interlocking your fingers. Use as many of these as possible; the effect of engaging multiple senses is alchemical and results in greater success in achieving your heart's desire.

You do not need to be still to be in a meditative state. You can practice visualization while involved in physical activities such as walking, doing the dishes, vacuuming, showering, dusting or working out. You can also use affirmations and mantras to help you focus your mind. Prayer beads, such as the Buddhist *mala*, which has 108 beads, are excellent to use for daily recitations of mantras or affirmations. With the mala, you touch one bead at a time as you internally repeat your statement, allowing you to repeat your affirmation 108 times without the conscious effort of counting. You can do this while walking or riding a stationary bike. This multimedia exercise is excellent for helping the brain anchor your vision in the new pathways. Following are some examples of self-culture affirmations. Make sure you are breathing slowly and evenly and truly feeling the words you are saying. If you use your childhood nickname in these affirmations, the energy of your words will target the child in you who has been keeping you paralyzed and stagnant in your nonself-culture life. In effect, you will essentially begin to heal the child within.

> I, __________ (childhood nickname), give myself permission to step into my authentic self.
>
> It is safe for me, __________ (childhood nickname), to be different from my family.
>
> The more I, __________ (childhood nickname), allow myself to be authentic, the more life conspires to create an authentic life for me.

When you visualize, let your mind see what your self-culture life might look like. If you have trouble doing this, then begin by musing about what it might feel like to live that kind of life. You might say to yourself, "I want to feel free." Then you might visualize yourself freely dancing or soaring above the clouds in a peaceful, flowing way. Or you might say, "I want to feel strong and powerful." Then you might visualize yourself with your spine like the trunk of an oak tree. Try to feel what it would be like to have a strong, oak-like core. Feel the very essence of the oak tree entering into your cells, making you feel strong and powerful. You might then add the vision of yourself encountering a strong wind that cannot topple you, no matter how hard it blows. It is then important to visualize yourself in real-life situations, in which you are free or strong or any other characteristic that illustrates your living a self-culture life. For example, you might see yourself freely expressing your opinions without feeling impacted by the other person's response, tone or mood. Or you might imagine yourself being a strong and empowered person in the face of a previously intimidating situation like public speaking, saying no, or confronting your boss.

It is important not to dilute the power you are harnessing when visualizing by sharing it with everyone you meet. There is a powerful energetic rule to follow if you want to harness and manifest the power of your intention: "to know, to will, to dare and to keep silent." When you are in the creation phase of this journey, you need pick only one or two cheerleaders to support you. To speak widely about the new territory you are trying to navigate will dilute the energy of your intention. Think of your intention as light energy. Light can be like a laser or a light bulb. Laser light has a tight beam that is so strong and concentrated that it can cut through concrete, whereas a light bulb's light is released in many directions and is very weak and diffuse. As you begin the process of finding your self-culture, be focused like the laser with your intention and visualizations; you will be more successful this way.

Clear Your Mind to Enable Change

It is also important to make sure you are creating your new neural pathways in an optimal environment; therefore, you have to become aware of the chatter that is going on largely in your subconscious and unconscious minds. What lives in your unconscious mind tends to control you more than what lives in your conscious mind. The more awareness you have of this, the better able you will be to make your desired changes.

It is also important not to reprimand yourself for having been weak, afraid or foolish. This work is not about self-criticism; it is about being compassionate with yourself regarding the state of mind you may find yourself in and realizing how magnificent you are, and then gently walking into a new way of being. No matter how broken you may feel, you are not damaged beyond repair. This work is walking a path of choice, but you cannot choose what you are not aware of.

I invite you to approach the journey of finding your self-culture as you would a plan to become physically fit. You need to work at it at least three times a week to stay fit; however, to truly change your level of fitness, you need to tackle it at least five times a week. This journey is no different; you need to commit to working on it at least five times a week to change your neural pathways, especially in the beginning. It can take many months, and sometimes years, of consistent work to transform the old into the new, but once the changes are more integrated into your being (i.e., the new neural pathways have transformed from footpaths to highways), you will be able to decrease the practice.

In addition, set reasonable goals around saying yes and no to people. Follow your own true desires and do things only when you truly want to. You will encounter difficult people who will not be happy with your choices, but they will be your greatest teachers. View them as opportunities to strengthen your resolve and further your growth. The idea is to feel deeply within your true self without the external input from other people or your mind's inner negative chatter.

Chapter Four

FAMILY-CULTURE CHALLENGES

Stop Emotional Dumpster Diving!

Daryl, an exceptionally intelligent man, had the terribly damaging habit of engaging in emotional relationships with women who were already involved with someone else. I call this "emotional dumpster diving." Daryl would invest in these women as if they were the most important people in his life, and he would repeat this over and over again, always ending up feeling used and abused—just a diversion on the side. Daryl's mother had been controlling and depressive. Her needs were the priority in his family, and in order to survive, Daryl learned to put himself on the back burner and make other people the priority in his life; this was normal behavior for him.

Emotional dumpster diving is when you treat yourself as if you deserve only garbage in life. Like dumpster diving in other people's trash for food, which may no longer be safe to eat, this can be risky. Following are some examples of emotional dumpster diving:

- Engaging in emotional affairs with people who are already in committed relationships
- Working in an abusive environment simply because it pays well
- Saying yes out of feelings of guilt
- Lying so as not to disappoint someone else

- Allowing others to manipulate you
- Always permitting your boundaries to be broken
- Never taking time for yourself to just be alone
- Being an "affirmation junkie"[1]
- Allowing other people's moods to affect your self-esteem
- Placating others to avoid abandonment

These behaviors prevent people from being in charge of their own lives and choices. They promote the destruction of self-esteem and feed depression and anxiety. They lack "emotional self-protection intelligence." They tend to settle for anyone who reaches out to them, accepting the attention because it came to them rather than being discerning and checking to see if the person is a good match. Intelligent people can do very dumb things; they aren't dumb, but they have not evolved emotionally to see themselves as valuable. Often these people grew up in families in which they had to switch off their own needs and sense of self-worth to survive the landmine of their family environment.

The family culture may have been one of constant criticism, fighting, addiction or not allowing anyone their feelings, so that family members had to repress their feelings and behave in a way that fit their family culture rather than being true to themselves. Children in families like this feel as though they are very low on the totem pole of priorities. They grow up not knowing how to feel because that muscle did not get used. As a result, they are unable to express themselves authentically, and as adults, they put their own needs very low on their list of priorities.

1 An "affirmation junkie" constantly needs affirmation from others; they live and die for others' approval, without which they have no sense of self-worth or purpose in life.

It is like growing up in an emotional desert—nurturing, affection, attention, affirmation, acknowledgment and acceptance are all lacking. The people coming out of these families end up emotionally starving and glomming onto anyone who is dishing out any of these precious commodities. They never were able to develop these important tools for themselves either. If we are not shown what to do when we are young, we have a hard time knowing what to do when we grow up. When we see love and healthy, loving relationships at home, it is like learning a language; the earlier we learn it, the easier it is to use later in life. As children, we are creatures of imitation, and if our parents do not model healthy, supportive behavior, we end up not being able to support ourselves emotionally. We end up going around trying on different relationships, seeing if, in a haphazard way, we can find the nurturing, affection, attention, affirmation, acknowledgment and acceptance that were missing from the family. It is a hit-and-miss proposition. And since our self-esteem is so low, there is a greater possibility that we will settle for anything that sort of feels good; in reality, however, such relationships are often dysfunctional and emotionally destructive.

Case Study: Fiona's Story

Fiona is a beautiful and musically talented woman who wanted to know how she could stop being so affected by her mother, who was depressed, critical and manipulative. With my help, Fiona learned to overcome the pattern of constantly trying to seek approval from her mother, who was not capable of giving anything to herself, let alone to her own daughter.

Fiona described her mother as being profoundly ill, and she felt that her attitude toward her had ruined her youth. She said her mother had no self-esteem; didn't know who she was; and was unhappy, blindfolded and stuck in old patterns. Her mother would use spiritual parables to point out how to be perfect. Fiona was born when her mother was about to leave her father, and she told Fiona that she had been an accident, and therefore made Fiona feel responsible for her unhappiness. Her mother acted as though she was jealous of Fiona's talent and natural happiness. Fiona was open and honest with her mother, telling her the truth about how she felt and what did and what didn't work for her. Her mother detested that Fiona expressed herself and tried to quash her as much as possible. Her mother used to belittle her in front of her family and friends. She mocked her and gossiped about her, telling them that Fiona had been such a difficult child and disclosing Fiona's private affairs to everybody.

When Fiona grew up, her mother didn't see her as the adult she was; she didn't respect her boundaries, and she was condescending and insulting toward her. When Fiona would tell her firmly to respect her boundaries, they would fight, and her mother would end up crying and saying how much she suffered because Fiona's behavior had ruined their relationship. Her mother would also try to make Fiona feel responsible for solving her problems of depression and insecurity, which she didn't have the courage to solve for herself. She would do this in a manipulative way, making Fiona feel guilty if she didn't help her because that is what a "good daughter" would do.

Fiona stopped talking to her mother for two years due to the effect her mother had on her. She thought that if her mother missed her, she would change, but she didn't. Because of her childhood experience, Fiona felt disconnected from her emotions. She had spent all those years loving her mother without understanding that her sense of self was being severely affected. She felt a combination of self-loathing and self-pity. She felt sorry for herself and wondered how she could find solace for the child inside her—the child who felt she wasn't worthy of love. Fiona wanted to know how she should behave in order to have a reasonable relationship with her mother. She wanted to be able to be confident and strong in her mother's presence.

Stop Being Your Parent's Parent!

In my sessions with Fiona, I first acknowledged that she had had an emotionally tough childhood and that her mother obviously had a lot of problems. I suggested that her mother might be depressed and that she also showed some characteristics of having a narcissistic personality or perhaps borderline personality disorder, as indicated by her persistent emotional instability and volatility.

Fiona felt she had been unloved, unheard, unseen, unwanted and manipulated. I told her I imagined seeing an immense tar-black, strong cord connected from her solar plexus to her mother, and even though she had tried to not be in contact with her mother, it seemed as though she had not really disconnected from her. Fiona didn't need to amputate her mother from her life; after all, her mother had given birth to her, but I suggested that she did need to detach herself from her and to individuate in a healthy way. A new normal had to be created, in which that cord that tied to the two together was cut. Fiona was still seeking approval from her mother, and I felt that this ought to be the first thing she needed to work on. I told her that her mother was never going to change because, in reality, people don't change unless they want to, and then put in the work to change. Change is difficult for those who work at it, so it is virtually impossible for those who do not.

Even though Fiona's mother seemed to be suffering, the familiarity of the way she was probably gave her some comfort.

The second thing Fiona had to do was to stop feeling responsible for the way her mother reacted. When Fiona tried to draw boundaries, such as asking her mother to respect her privacy and stop gossiping about her to others, her mother would be hurt and she would cry, playing the role of the victim. As a result, any message Fiona was trying to relay to her was lost. I explained to Fiona that she could draw a boundary, but she was not responsible for her mother's reaction, and she needed to stop thinking she was in control of her mother's reactions. Fiona's task was to try to disconnect from her mother's reactions so she could stop seeing herself through her mother's eyes because, in fact, her mother wasn't seeing the true Fiona. She was seeing her daughter through the filter of her own distorted vision, and what she saw was her own dark side.

Fiona was probably right when she said she thought her mother was jealous of her freedom, beauty and talents, but she had to understand that her mother could not be consoled. I asked her why she wanted a relationship with her mother, and, of course, the main reason was that she was her mother, which is reasonable. However, I explained to Fiona that she had to make a substantial shift in the way she related to her. I knew that Fiona would suffer tremendously, mostly from guilt, if she didn't see her mother at all, so I suggested that she needed to see less of her mother, but not amputate her, preferably only once a month for an hour or two, perhaps over a meal or in an activity such as shopping. She could check in on her by phone once a week to make sure she was all right, but she had to be disciplined about this and make the communications short and to the point. I advised her to establish a disciplined pattern of seeing her mother that served her own needs—not her mother's; this way she could have peace of mind regarding her mother's well-being, while at the same time avoid destructive patterns of communication with her mother. This would be the new normal that Fiona would establish in order to have a healthy relationship with her mother and with herself. I explained to Fiona that her mother was like a wounded lion. Yes, the lion needs to be cared for, but not at the peril of the caretaker, who has to use extreme caution when caring for the wounded animal. To feed the lion, the caretaker must slide the bowl of food to it with a long stick in order to maintain a safe distance. Fiona needed to protect herself whenever she was in contact with her mother. She could not go to her without having the motivation, and the clear intention, to make herself and her well-being a priority in the dynamic between herself and her mother.

I also advised Fiona to protect her privacy and not reveal so much about her life to her mother. If her mother didn't have the information, she wouldn't be able to share it with the world. Fiona also needed to stop trying to tell her mother what to do or not do. The only right Fiona had was to communicate to her mother what her boundaries were when she felt they were being crossed. People who don't want to be taught will not learn, and the teacher appears when the student is ready. Fiona's mother was not ready to be taught—or to be shown.

In Fiona's case, I was particularly concerned that she had already been damaged by this relationship, which is why I wanted her to maintain clear boundaries in her relationship with her mother going forward. Fiona had already tried to break away completely, and it didn't help, but when she took this disciplined approach, she was able to recover and become stronger. Over time, she was able to completely cut the cords of the dysfunctional connection, while still maintaining a relationship with her mother. But the connection was now very different. She no longer sought her mother's approval, or even love and compassion from her. Fiona grew to understand that her mother was not capable of giving this to her; she wasn't even capable of giving it to herself. She stopped trying to pick cherries from the apple tree, because they were not there.

The Collateral Damage of the Narcissistic Parent

There is significant evidence that indicates that children who suffer emotional abuse during childhood are more likely to suffer from depression, anxiety and post-traumatic stress disorder (PTSD) later in life.[2,3] As such, a family culture that involves a parent with a narcissistic personality (NP) is extremely challenging for the children. Often abuse occurs at the hands of a narcissist parent. Because this parent has to be the main person with the biggest emotions in the room, the children grow up always deferring to that parent. They are not allowed to feel or have problems, only the parent can, and they constantly have to fight for attention.

People with NP have a strong sense of superiority and have difficulty with any kind of criticism. They think they are better than anyone else, and they are self-centered and self-involved in the extreme. They often go back and forth from behaving like a tyrant to behaving like a victim, and they use manipulation to get what

2 Philip Spinhoven et al., "The Specificity of Childhood Adversities and Negative Life Events across the Life Span to Anxiety and Depressive Disorders," *Journal of Affective Disorders* 126, no. 1-2 (2010): 103–112. doi: 10.1016/j.jad.2010.02.132.

3 Harriet L. MacMillan et al., "Childhood Abuse and Lifetime Psychopathology in a Community Sample," *The American Journal of Psychiatry* 158, no. 11 (2001): 1878–1883. doi: 10.1176/appi.ajp.158.11.1878.

they want. We can all be self-involved at times, and this is normal, but when extreme, the behavior is volatile and abusive. These people are dramatic and emotional; they're up, they're down, they're depressed, they're screaming, they're yelling. Their problems and feelings are at the center of the room, and nobody else's matter to them. These people also have a difficult time in relationships. They often feel victimized and that their needs are all that matter. They are unable to empathize with others, and the ability to empathize with and have compassion for another person is a strong indication of mental, emotional and spiritual health.

Children of narcissists generally feel there's something missing within them. In addition, they do not know themselves—who they really are, or what their feelings are. In their family cultures, the parents' feelings have always been front and center, while their own feelings had to take a back seat. Often the narcissistic parent will mock and belittle the children when they show their feelings, or interrupt them when they're speaking, so that their ability to communicate is hampered significantly. As a result, children of narcissists grow up feeling as though they are outsiders in their own families. Their feelings of emotional abandonment lead them to become people-pleasers, sometimes sabotaging themselves to please others. They are not interested in taking care of themselves because, as children, they had to do whatever was right for the parent, which meant that they lost their sense of what was right for themselves.

Children of narcissistic parents also grow up having no idea of their own needs, and in a bid to survive they may imitate their parents' way of being in order to find a voice for themselves. They learn that the only way to be heard is to fall into the family-culture way of being, which results only in wreaking havoc in their adult relationships.

If you were the child of a narcissistic parent or parents, I want to acknowledge that you have survived a difficult childhood, and you have to watch for a few things. First, be careful that you are not attracting narcissists into your life. In an effort to try to fix your parents in some way, or to understand them, you may bring other similar personality disorders into your life.

Second, be careful not to become a narcissist yourself. You need to be self-aware and also realize that you are no longer at the mercy of your parents' narcissism. Being self-aware means being present in any given moment. If you are in an argument with someone, ask yourself, "Am I being reasonable?" or, "Am I being overly demanding?" You can also ask yourself if you are in a relationship that is just like that of your parents, and if you are, take stock. I encourage you to keep a journal and make notes on everything you notice that could indicate that you are narcissistic yourself, or that you are in a relationship with a narcissist. Observe whether you are depressed and don't know who you are or your own voice, or what you want and need in your relationships. Allow your wants and needs to come to the surface, whisper them to yourself, and soon they will become louder. Self-acknowledgment, self-compassion, self-love and self-empathy are the beginning of healing, and the more you voice your wants and needs, the more you will become the balanced adult you seek to become.

Chapter Five

FAMILY CULTURE: GUILT AND ANGER

Guilt and anger are two of the biggest culprits in keeping you from being yourself!

The "Zombie Land" of Guilt

One big obstacle to being yourself is the profound guilt that arises at the prospect of uttering the truths that come from the bottom of your longing soul. Family culture can teach us how to feel guilt. This extraordinarily toxic emotion has its roots in positive emotions, such as empathy, compassion and the need to help and belong. However, the emotions that were once good and healthy turn into a poisonous potion of manipulation that is almost impossible to get rid of without mammoth efforts. Guilt is destructive and creates profound feelings of self-loathing.

Guilt can make people react to life in a zombie-like way. When I think of guilt, I have an image of zombies walking around, arms outstretched and eyes glazed over, motivated by the need to kill the guilt at all costs. They need to do whatever it takes to stop the guilt—usually by doing what other people want them to do, without any regard for themselves. The impulse is so strong that it takes over their whole being. When you are a slave to guilt, it's as if you're living in "Zombie Land"!

Guilt is the best and most effective way to control people, countries, voting decisions and more because it promotes fear. The perpetrators concoct crazy scenarios in the minds of their "victims" about the terrible damage that will occur if they do not do what they are asking or demanding. Families can also employ guilt to manipulate family members to fit into the family culture in the way they are, what they do and what they say. Because we don't want to see ourselves as terrible people, we make decisions that are contrary to what would make us happy. It's all about the other person and not about us. In this situation, we learn that our feelings are less valuable than those of the person who wants to control us. We ignore our own feelings and desires so as not to hurt the other person and, presumably, to make them happy. Guilt, which holds us back from being ourselves, is a control tactic used consciously or unconsciously to gain power over us. The abhorrent manipulation that gives rise to feelings of guilt if we do not fall into line is universally recognized as a terrible thing, and yet it is used ubiquitously.

Case Study: Ruth's Journey through Guilt

Having grown up half Catholic and half Jewish myself, I can speak to the culture of guilt that comes from either half! Today, Eastern spirituality is what resonates more deeply within me, and so I no longer practice either one; however, I joke that Catholic guilt is about sex, and Jewish guilt is about food. On a more serious note, guilt of any kind is very destructive.

Ruth, a wonderful person and the daughter of a survivor, told me that the messaging she received at home was that she did not feel bad enough for having survived the holocaust. Her family culture was driven by the guilt of surviving. It was her family members' duty to be the best at everything because they had survived. They had to be the best at business, at school and in physical appearance. It was not okay to just relax and do nothing; they had to constantly be achieving or producing something. Her issues were ensconced in obsessive overachievement.

Ruth landed in my office burned out and just this side of a mild heart attack—a wake-up call, she said. I told her it was a gift from the universe to bring her to the challenge of finding her self-culture. Clearly, her family culture did not work for her! In fact, to continue down that road would practically have been suicide. Her life was unmanageable, and the effect on her health was a message saying, "Stop the madness of relentlessly doing and trying to achieve—now!" However, she had no idea about how to relax.

Ruth was attracted to the type of work that I do in my office because just talking with a therapist had not helped her; in fact, it was hindering her from shifting her behavior patterns. Sitting and talking made her antsy. She could not focus on the session for longer than a minute at a time. She would refuse to turn her BlackBerry off; the most she would concede was to set it to vibrate. But the second she felt the vibration, if she didn't answer it, she would feel so profoundly guilty that she *had* to answer. She was like a zombie, unable to defer the call to a later time. She had to jump *now* to find out what was wanted of her.

I told Ruth that to develop new neural pathways that corresponded with new behavior, she had to practice a new behavior often, and these therapy sessions were a good place to start. I began to do body-centered work with her, and this required her to have her electronic device turned off completely so that the atmosphere would be quiet and peaceful. Her nervous system was in constant fight-or-flight mode; in other words, her sympathetic nervous system, which activates the body's response to stress, was being overactivated by never-ending demands that she felt she had to act on in order to survive; she was in survival mode all the time, and this was her "normal." Ruth metabolized the concept that she needed to always be on the move and doing something to feel valuable. She had to earn her place on the planet; she had no right to just be. In effect, her parasympathetic nervous system, which activates the body's relaxation response, was turned off. Her brain messaging was "I gotta run, move, do—or else!" But she was just following her family culture; she knew no other way.

During the bodywork sessions with Ruth, I encouraged her to talk. Her eyes were covered with a flaxseed pillow so she could go deeply within herself. This helped her to visualize, and she was able to recall distant memories of herself as a child watching TV after school, only to be scolded and criticized for being lazy. She also remembered being cruelly bullied by her brother, who told on her when she dared to sit down to make crafts or do anything creative. "This is a waste of time," her parents would scream. "You can't make a living as an artist, so you better not even think about it." Remembering this, the lightbulb came on for her. She felt a profound grief, which had been deeply lodged in her body, rise to the surface. Tears of deep sadness poured out. She remembered begging her parents for painting lessons, but they had refused categorically to allow her to do so on the grounds that it would be a colossal waste of time for a member of their family, whose mission it was to prove they deserved to be alive. But she was just a young girl, wanting to explore her artistic abilities, which her teacher had complimented her on. When Ruth remembered this, she felt a sense of guilt that she might be betraying her parents. She almost whispered as she told me the story, as if she were afraid her parents might hear us.

Ruth also recalled walking home from school alone and marveling at the sky, the clouds, the trees, the leaves—all the colors of nature. She fantasized about painting everything she saw. She dreamed in color and sensed that her soul wanted to express these dreams on canvas. She then remembered her older brother coming along as she was slowly walking home. Her brother, who had been schooled in the same family-culture ways, felt he had an obligation to uphold the parental mandate of productivity first, at all costs, and so he chastised his little sister for taking too long to walk home. He also told on her, which resulted in her parents' deciding that it was essential that they cut this artistic thing at its root. They made sure she was enrolled in after-school courses in math, science and business, and that her teacher knew what they wanted for their daughter. Ruth's parents belittled her so often that she finally made herself shut off all her artistic inclinations. She wanted to make her parents proud, and the only way to do this was to betray herself.

After we had worked together for a time, Ruth was able to bring down her guilt levels bit by bit. She gave herself permission to explore painting and drawing. For the first time in her life, she began to have a sense of freedom of her own expression. This feeling became strong enough to help her overcome the feelings of guilt that once trapped her. She showed me some of her drawings, and I thought they were wonderful, but at first she would point out what she perceived were imperfections in her work. Eventually, she realized that art is a process; she didn't have to be perfect at it, and she knew she would improve in time. The fact that she had begun to individuate with her self-expression was of value unto itself. She cherished her journey toward living her own self-culture because she realized she could be a better daughter, mother and wife if she cared for her own needs first. Overall, her health also improved significantly.

So often I see people in my practice who become profoundly depressed and anxious because of the guilt they feel when they begin to individuate and honor their own self-culture. They become paralyzed and unable to move past their feelings of guilt for desiring to be authentic. The conflict between what their souls want and what their family culture wants is so great that by the time they come to see me, they feel completely taken down.

Case Study: Breaking Free of Family Control

Beatrice, an accomplished engineer, was stuck, unable to live her life independently from her family. She was on the edge of losing her new boyfriend, with whom she was falling in love. She dreamt of a new life of independence that included a good love partnership. She came to see me with the intention of understanding why she was so angry, sad and unable to stop sabotaging her relationship. She was plagued by unrelenting jealousy and suspicion regarding her boyfriend.

As the therapy evolved, we learned a great deal about her family dynamic. She was the soul financial provider for her mother, father and adult brother. Because of circumstances, her parents were unable to make ends meet. They received some money from the government, but it wasn't enough to pay for a lifestyle that included their large house. They refused to downsize to a less expensive home because they were completely enslaved by their feelings of guilt about their adult son, who was unable to support himself financially. This son was an unmotivated TVaholic who worked as a part-time mover, even though, at his parents' expense, he had a college diploma in business. Her parents were male-centric, always valuing boys over girls and enabling their son, never demanding anything of him that remotely resembled being responsible for himself. He was treated with kid gloves, whereas Beatrice was expected to keep up her "duty" of supporting everyone without protest. When she suggested that her parents move into a one-bedroom condo, they said that would mean leaving their son on the streets, and they would chastise her for being insensitive. Her parents' constant demands were made in a subtle, manipulative, passive-aggressive manner, creating such feelings of guilt in Beatrice that she was enslaved by their expectations.

Guilt deprives a person of being able to discern what is best for themselves. Beatrice sustained a complete brainwashing so that her feelings of guilt had such power over her that she gave up on her dreams of traveling, living on her own, saving money for her future or having a life and family of her own. She was thirty-eight years old, but her behavior with her boyfriend was like that of a teenager. She lived at home, and her mom did all the laundry and cooking. The family dynamic was stagnant, frozen in a time when parents governed the lives of their daughters, no matter how old they were.

Over time, Beatrice also became a "comfort junkie"—a coping mechanism to be able to accept what she felt she couldn't change.

She was used to living at home and participating in the family routine. She truly felt that she belonged there, and, above all, she felt safe. She mused, "Why bother traveling? It would only cause Mom and Dad pain. Why rock the boat? I would only become depressed with the guilt of causing my parents pain." In one session, she blurted out, "I would sacrifice myself for my parents. They gave me everything. I can't imagine what I would do without them!" Yet she was deeply unhappy, and her anger over not being able to move forward in her life was putting her in danger of ruining the one good thing in her life—her relationship with her boyfriend.

I pressed her to give me some examples of her parents' doing everything for her. I asked her who had paid for her education, her car, her clothes, her books and all her other needs since she was sixteen. She paused to think and then quietly responded with sadness in her voice, "I did." She also affirmed that her parents had paid for all of these things for her brother.

At this point, Beatrice began the slow process of realizing where some of her anger was coming from. This is the first step for many people in breaking down their feelings of guilt. They need to become their own advocates and begin the immense process of making themselves their priority and feeling compassion for themselves. They need to work on not allowing other people's agendas impact them. It isn't healthy to always see yourself through the eyes and feelings of someone else, and yet this is ingrained in many of us, and so it requires a lot of work to overcome the programming.

As Beatrice began to make new decisions for herself, such as moving out, setting up a more reasonable budget for her parents and traveling, her feelings of guilt would definitely make their presence known; however, she slowly began to make real progress. Despite her feelings of guilt, she chose to move step by step toward her self-culture until she was no longer paralyzed. Her life slowly began to become more independence-oriented. She stopped projecting her anger onto her boyfriend, and so that relationship improved as well. Her sense of joy increased as she tasted her freedom more often. This started to become her new normal, which she chose to protect. Her journey toward living her self-culture evolved with choices that she consistently made to honor herself.

Guilt versus Regret

I invite you to consider the notions of guilt and regret. These two concepts live on opposite sides of a spectrum. On the one hand, guilt can turn you into a zombie, where you are enslaved by it. You have nowhere to go but down. You have no choice but to try to quell the most painful feelings in your heart and soul. Guilt conjures images of the horrors you are inflicting on someone else. You are the bad one. If you try to make yourself a priority, then you are a terrible person, daughter, son, friend, partner, mother, father or employee. You have no concept of what self-value, let alone self-culture, is. Your self-esteem is down the tube. Your sense of who you truly are is off-kilter. You are drowning in self-criticism. You are in a lose-lose situation. You cannot experience personal growth or make any progress when you are suffering from and motivated by guilt.

On the other hand, regret allows you to feel compassion for the other person and have a sense of self as well. For example, you might say to yourself, "I regret that I can no longer help that person in the way I used to, but it doesn't make me a bad person. The other person's needs are important, but I can attend to them only if I am full and taken care of. It is unfortunate that what that person wants and needs conflicts with my real self, but I need to draw some personal boundaries at the moment." You have a sense of your limitations. You are not living your life as a martyr and at the mercy of someone else's wants and needs. Also with regret, there is a thought process that allows you to see the issue from a broader perspective so that you can learn something from the event. I call this "transcendence thinking." That is, you are able to see the lesson in the event versus being wrapped up in a myopic perspective in which you do not see the forest for the trees. With regret, you get to see what is motivating you versus being unconsciously at the mercy of guilt. With regret, you give yourself permission to fill your own cup first, and only then do you give to others from the overflow. You can live with regret without being crushed by guilt, and this can be the beginning of finding your own innate self-culture.

Anger and the Cycle of Self-Denial

The cycle of self-denial chart (opposite) illustrates how denying your needs can lead to anger. So often I have seen people who are so used to not asking for what they need—and don't even acknowledge that they have needs—that they reach a state of self-denial. "I don't have needs," they say, and usually they can pull this off, but at great cost to themselves.

At first they keep their needs to themselves and don't express them to anyone. They consider it selfish to be thinking of what they want. Their needs are low on their priority lists, and if they do express their needs, they feel guilty and ashamed. But, of course, as time progresses, their basic human needs—to be seen, heard and understood, and to feel fulfilled—start to bleed through. They begin to experience a sense of incongruity—a fight between "I don't want to admit that I have needs" and "I have needs."

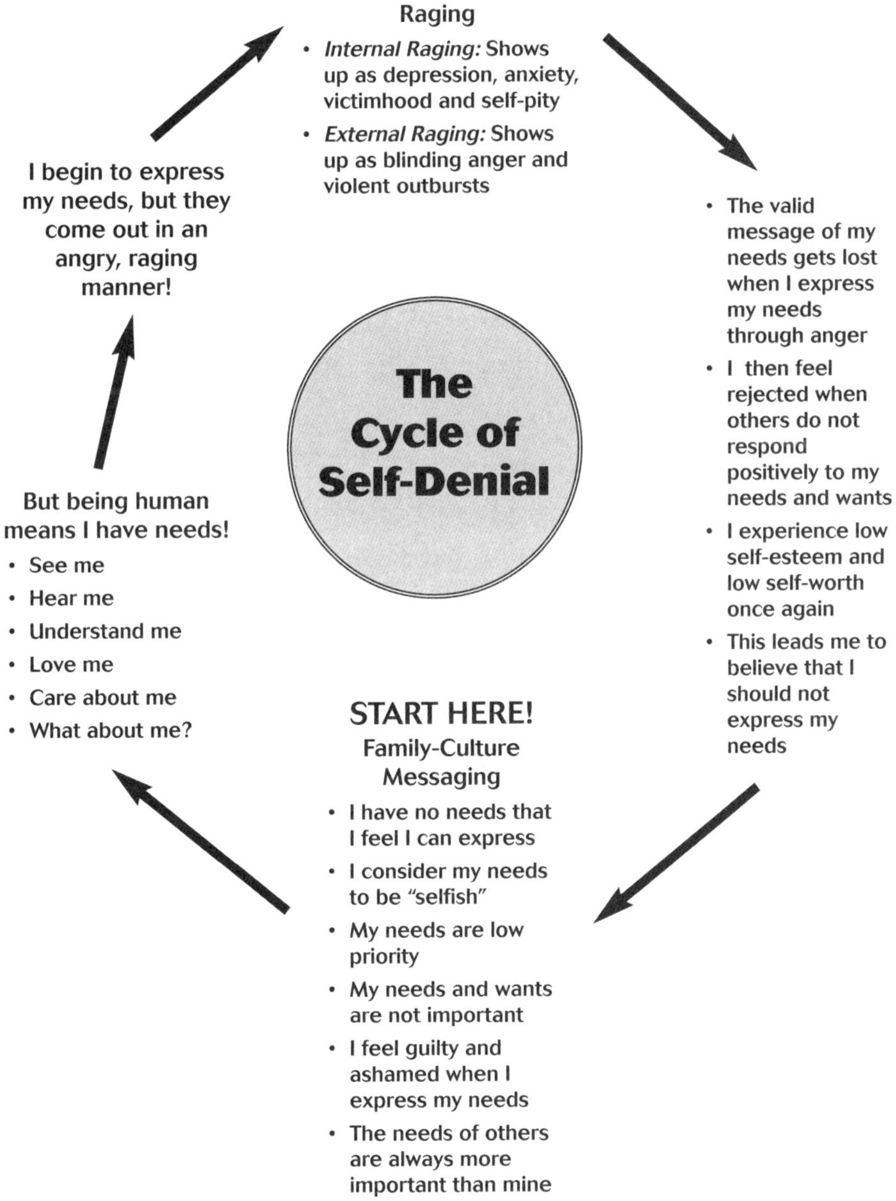
Raging
• Internal Raging: Shows up as depression, anxiety, victimhood and self-pity
• External Raging: Shows up as blinding anger and violent outbursts
• The valid message of my needs gets lost when I express my needs through anger
• I then feel rejected when others do not respond positively to my needs and wants
• I experience low self-esteem and low self-worth once again
• This leads me to believe that I should not express my needs
START HERE!
Family-Culture Messaging
• I have no needs that I feel I can express
• I consider my needs to be "selfish"
• My needs are low priority
• My needs and wants are not important
• I feel guilty and ashamed when I express my needs
• The needs of others are always more important than mine
But being human means I have needs!
• See me
• Hear me
• Understand me
• Love me
• Care about me
• What about me?
I begin to express my needs, but they come out in an angry, raging manner!
The Cycle of Self-Denial

What usually occurs next is that they either internalize their rage or express it outwardly. Internal raging often results in depression, anxiety and a deep sense of dissatisfaction with themselves and their lives, which drags down their self-esteem. External raging is exactly that: anger expressed outwardly, often in violent outbursts; it is frustration from a place deep inside that has come to the boiling point. Whether their rage is internalized or expressed outwardly, these people send out undesirable energy, and they are difficult to be around. The fact that they have needs gets lost in their rage, and the world responds to them by saying, "I don't want to have anything to do with you," and as a result, their needs are never met, and they feel rejected and abandoned, they lose friends, become lonely, and their self-esteem and feelings of self-worth hit rock bottom. Often when a person's self-esteem is lowered, they say things like "I don't deserve to have needs," "I don't have value" and "I'm not worth much." So guess what? The cycle of self-denial begins all over again.

How to Stop the Cycle of Self-Denial

If you are caught in the cycle of self-denial, then you must first know that it is right, good and healthy to have needs, and then to find peaceful, loving, fair and kind ways to express those needs. Keep a journal so that you can record when you feel a need for something. Step into your adult self and give yourself permission to have needs. The needs do not have to be obscured by inner or outer rage. Even if you have been trained by your family culture or through bad experiences not to express your needs, it is important that you know that you have a right to have your needs satisfied!

At the same time, though you have a right to express your needs, it is not other people's responsibility to fulfill them. It is your right to be vulnerable and make requests, and you can learn to express your needs in a calm, fair, kind and loving way so you are heard, and not leave them buried inside, causing damage, or let them out in fits of anger that only leave you feeling guilty; however, you also need to be able to fulfill your own needs as much as possible.

It can be helpful if you understand how you got caught up in the cycle of self-denial. Some conditions in our lives can promote the denial of our needs. In some families, there is a long-standing, multigenerational pattern of deprivation of one's emotional needs. Patterns of high drama, narcissistic behavior, addiction and emotional blackmail, where guilt and shame are the commodities on offer when someone expresses their needs, may be etched into the family culture. In such a situation, people learn that to have needs is to be disappointed. Also, as a child, a person might have been caught up in the role of the peacemaker or the diplomat in a family of conflicting sides. The child learns that, because of the chaos around them, it is not advantageous to be perceived as high-maintenance. However, in reality, as children, we are all about needs: Feed me, see me, love me, change me. Me, me, me. When children are deprived of their needs, they metabolize the pattern of not expressing them as they grow up. In time, they are not even conscious of their own needs; they are buried way down in the subconscious realm, waiting to explode on the scene.

Once you understand the cycle and its causes, and that you have the right to have your needs heard, the lessons on finding your self-culture in this book can help you break out of the vicious circle of self-denial and learn to fulfill your own needs.

Moving Beyond Anger toward Your Parents

I see many people who have suffered for so long with unresolved anger toward their parents, wishing their upbringing had been different. As adults, they seem to fear that not suffering would be tantamount to condoning their parents' treatment of them, and so their anger solidifies and they project their unresolved issues onto their partners and friends.

Case Study: Finding Love in the Right Places

Mary, a woman of thirty-five, came to see me because she couldn't break the pattern of attracting the wrong kind of men into her life. She grew up in a very difficult family home. As a child, she experienced an emotionally withholding mother who was extremely manipulative, and worst of all, she withheld her love when Mary displeased her. Her father was also distant and emotionally unavailable. He was the kind of man who didn't show emotion or affection. He was authoritarian and lacked empathy. Mary was a very lonely and sad child.

As an adult, Mary found herself repeating a series of relationships with men, onto whom she projected her anger toward her parents. She was unconsciously attracting men, who, like her parents, were emotionally unavailable and didn't show their emotions. Because she hadn't resolved her past, she kept repeating the pattern, and she was unable to move out of the cycle. (Madness has been defined as doing the same thing over and over again and expecting a different result!)

Her relationships followed a familiar trajectory every time. She would fall for the wrong guy; he wouldn't make her a priority in his life; she would begin to cling to him so she would not feel abandoned and disappointed. She often felt as though she wasn't doing enough, and so she would compensate by trying to please him in order to get some affection and love from the relationship. Inevitably, her boyfriend would find this tiresome, she would become frustrated, her buried anger and pain from her childhood experience would surface and a fight would ensue.

With every failed relationship, Mary's pain and depression would increase. The deprived child within her was running the show. She was seeking love in all the wrong places, and yet her unconscious drive to be loved by that particular type of person always seduced her in a way that she could not control. It was literally acting like a drug within her. The passion that the drama of these relationships offered her was like crack cocaine; it would initially send her into a haze of joy, which would only turn into a desperation that seemed to shut her adult self right up and empower her hurt child to do its damage.

Mary asked, "Why am I so seduced by this kind of person? How do I break the pattern of projecting my family issues onto my adult relationships?" I told her that the answer was in the unresolved hurt of the deprived child who was running the show. The only way for her to break the cycle of dysfunction was to make it her number one priority to tend to the hurting child within. Only then would the child settle down. Mary needed to show the child that she would make better, more self-nurturing choices for herself. This would be the only way the child would stop acting out with the bad choices Mary had been making and begin to trust that good things can come from healthy choices.

Through the visualization exercise in appendix II, "Reparenting Yourself," Mary was eventually able to do the opposite of what she would normally have done. First, she had to create a loving, compassionate and forgiving relationship with herself, and with repetition of this exercise, at the first sign of an emotionally unavailable and withholding man, she was soon able to act counter-intuitively, and instead of grasping for affection in a place that would surely disappoint her, she did the opposite: She refused to invest emotionally in such a person. In this way, she showed her inner child that there was another way to get the love she needed. This child knew only the emotional patterns of her upbringing, and the familiar gave her a sense of comfort, however misdirected. Mary had to reeducate the child within in order to create new neural pathways that would link the drive for love with healthier choices. In time, Mary learned to say "run, don't walk!" in the face of emotional abuse or emotional withholding. A new vibration took over her being, and she began to attract the kind of relationships she craved.

Remember, your inner child needs repetition to unlearn old patterns that surface in your adult life. Hurt and deprived children only want love and affection and to feel they are a priority in their parents' eyes. If dysfunctional love is all children experience, then that kind of love is normal to them. If, like Mary, you are suffering because you did not get what you wanted and needed from your parents, and you are carrying the baggage of hurt and anger into your adult life, you may find that by repeating the reparenting exercise in appendix II, your life will transform!

Chapter Six

SHAME, SHAME, SHAME!

In addition to guilt and anger, shame also prevents you from embracing and living your self-culture. Shame is a like a disease that progressively destroys your life. It makes its way insidiously into your life and brings you down. Those who did not grow up in a culture of shaming behavior are able to recognize it, and then avoid it, whereas those for whom shame was a fundamental part of their family culture have a hard time identifying it as something they should steer clear of. Because shame is ingrained in their family dynamics, it is metabolized and seems normal. In fact, often it is sought out like an addictive substance and integrated as the normal way of being treated and of treating others.

Many people who are not able to find their self-culture and experience their own ways of being have likely grown up in families in which the main method of communication was coercion through shaming.

What Do Shaming and Shame Look Like?

People who communicate through shaming may say things such as "What is wrong with you?" "How can you be so stupid?" "Why can't you be more like [so and so]?" "You make me sick!" "If you do [this], then I will love you" and "You are never going to get a man if you look like that!" It is a constant tearing away at any self-value through verbal abuse, name calling, emotional abandonment, criticism and mocking. And, of course, it may not always be as obvious; they may simply not allow the person to have feelings, opinions or problems, or make mistakes, by criticizing and judging them or rejecting them by giving them the silent treatment. As a result, the recipient of this treatment is rendered insecure, self-doubting and self-deprecating.

Adults who grew up always being shamed end up judging themselves and others. In that paradigm, it would be wrong for them to accept themselves as they are. Why would they want to accept someone who had regularly been so profoundly rejected by their home tribes—their own families. At the same time, it is normal for them to have wanted to fit in with their families—to belong, to be a part of a group. Families who use shame often have this double-edged sword—on the one hand, they use shame to communicate with one another, and on the other, family members can feel a part of the family unit as long as they conform to the shaming behavior of the family culture. This shaming behavior, coupled with the need to belong, can cause a person to be willingly drawn to dysfunctional relationships.

Case Study: Rose's Family Culture of Shaming

Rose, a high-functioning professional, came to see me because her twelve-year marriage was in crisis; she was on the brink of separation from her husband, and it was affecting their nine-year-old daughter. She and her husband had become antagonistic toward one another, and she had recently become drawn to another man. She had so far had no physical intimacy outside her partnership with her husband, but the situation was getting dicey, and she felt she was at the tipping point. This extramarital relationship was an escape for her and a healing respite from the bitterness at home. She was tempted to leave her marriage to pursue this less-than-healthy relationship.

Rose told me that her husband was always criticizing her in a shaming way. He would call her names, such as "bitch." They would swear at one another when they fought, which was very disrespectful, and they often fought in front of their daughter. Rose also criticized her husband, saying he spent too much time on the computer, didn't pull his weight with the household chores and was too lax in the parenting of their daughter. She said he controlled the home dynamic by insulting and denigrating her personality every time she had anything negative to say about anything. She said he was jealous of how much attention she gave their child. This was evidenced by his storming around in a tantrum when she was giving their daughter individual time. (I observed that Rose was an overfunctioner, and this behavior only exacerbated her perception of her husband as being an underfunctioner. Overfunctioners tend to see others as underfunctioners, whether they are or are not.)

Even though things were going from bad to worse, Rose and her husband were both too afraid to leave the relationship. Each of them threatened to leave, but neither ever followed through.

In the meantime, their daughter was acting out, throwing temper tantrums, destroying her room, being aggressive at home and at school and, the most heart-wrenching of all, being self-critical and obviously feeling insecure. Rose and her husband habitually yelled at their daughter in response to her behavior, shaming her to get her to stop, which, of course, was to no avail. This was the breaking point that motivated Rose to seek out therapy.

Rose's Family of Origin

Rose's family culture was fraught with shaming dynamics, which she had normalized. She grew up in a home where the yelling of expletives was commonplace. Anytime anyone made a mistake, an uncaring, personality-destroying barrage would ensue. Complete intolerance of one another was the name of the game. Those who made mistakes had to be prepared for battle. In addition, Rose's father was a perfectionist, who would regularly set the stage so that the siblings had to compete for his affection and attention.

Rose's Healing Journey

In my sessions with Rose, we began by working together to help her become aware of the dynamics of her family of origin, which she had normalized. Her natural instinct was to fiercely defend her family, but her defensiveness was the result of her not acknowledging how she had felt growing up. She seemed to have blocked those feelings entirely.

I had Rose lie down comfortably with her eyes closed, and while doing a combination of talk and energy work, she began to explore her childhood. She soon began to see that her family dynamic had been one of painful, shame-based communication. She had difficulty relating to the word *shame*. After all, she was a high-functioning, well-paid professional. "How can I be filled with shame?" she asked.

Rose realized that throughout her childhood she had always felt that she wasn't good enough. She didn't even know what activities she wanted to take part in, what she desired or how to behave in a style that was her own. As we explored more deeply, she realized that her husband's behavior was the mirror image of that of her family. As painful as this was for Rose, I told her that she now had an opportunity to heal this part of herself and stop this family dynamic from being passed down to her daughter. With her new awareness—and the decision to change her behavior—she could stop the dysfunction in its tracks.

Rose realized that she needed to stop seeking approval from others as a way to feel good about herself. Shame has a way of robbing us of our self-esteem, so we need others to validate us. However, we can't really depend on others for this because it is a precarious place to put our self-esteem; they may help us initially, but it will not last. Rose's overfunctioning behavior was also a means for her to boost her self-esteem, but it eventually turned to resentment over doing more than she actually wanted to do, and she realized she had to work to stop this behavior. Her way of relating to her husband and the new man in her life was also her way of building up her feelings of self-worth, but self-worth gained in this way is superficial and does not last either. It is soon depleted, and she would have to go back often for another hit to replenish the high feeling. Overfunctioning, constantly finding solutions to other people's problems and seeking approval are all behaviors that originate from the shame-based feelings of profound insecurity and low self-esteem. The boost in feelings of self-worth achieved by these behaviors is also addictive because the good feelings are never quite sated and require more and more to be built up.

As Rose's therapy progressed, she began to stop nagging and belittling her husband and engaging him in name-calling fights. She started to realize that just because she didn't agree with him, it didn't mean that he was wrong. She came to understand that shaming her husband in order to coerce him into changing was only distracting herself from dealing with her own issues. Her preoccupation with him only served to make her feel self-righteous and justified in criticizing and judging him.

Our sessions included meditative visualization, which included Rose's making regular contact with her inner self. And to enhance her self-care, Rose also started taking a meditation course to help her become more introspective so she could truly understand herself and her motivations.

By the end of her therapy sessions with me, Rose understood how she had also been shaming her daughter to make her obey her, but, of course, this had not worked. Instead, Rose began to reward her daughter for good behavior and ignore the bad. She also found that allowing the natural consequences of mistakes to take their course was much more effective in bringing about change in her husband and daughter than using shame to criticize them could ever have been. For example, when her husband forgot to buy tickets in advance for a concert the family was to attend, Rose didn't shame him; instead, she let the consequence of their not being able to go to the concert teach him that he had to rely on himself rather than depend on her to look after the details. He felt he had let the family down. It was a self-learning lesson for him as he felt the consequence of his lapse. Similarly, rather than shaming her daughter for not handing in a school project on time, Rose let her feel the consequences and get a bad grade; this then became a learning opportunity for her daughter. Her family also became less nasty toward one another, and Rose's extramarital relationship faded and never got off the ground. Rose and her husband also began to see me regularly for couple's therapy. The shaming wasn't completely gone, but it was on its way out.

Chapter Seven

THE HURT CHILD AND THE CRITICAL PARENT

The journey toward self-culture begins with healing the hurt child within that you have carried with you into adulthood. How do you heal that wounded child? How do you master going beyond what you have been taught to do repeatedly, either by observing the behavior or by having it drilled into you ad nauseam?

When a client enters my office, I ask, "What is not working for you in your life? What do you want to change?" The client is usually quick to reply. He or she will say, "I don't know, but what I do know is that I want to be happy," or, "I want to feel different from the way I feel now," or, "I want to have better relationships."

To illuminate where therapy might lead them, I say that therapy is not about changing who you are; it is about becoming more of who you really are, which is what I am also teaching in this book. The therapy is not meant to change you into someone else; it is work that helps to unearth the authentic you—the you before you had to armor yourself for protection. The authentic you who was there before you underwent a trauma that forced you into abandoning your true self, which, in turn, led you to convince yourself that who you are is not okay.

Change requires three main elements:

1. **Awareness** to see with clarity what is truly going on
2. **Willingness** to do whatever it takes to move into a shift
3. **Courage** to face this sometimes immensely challenging process toward authenticity

So often we carry heavy baggage from the past with us. Even though the baggage is from another time, it often runs the show. And sometimes it ruins the show! We have become so used to carrying this baggage that we do not fully realize it is even there. It is like an amputated arm that we constantly feel as phantom pain; an itch we cannot scratch; a pain we cannot diminish. We sense it, but we are not fully aware of it. When we look deeply into this baggage, we see that its contents are wrapped up in two distinct voices, or states of being, that seem to be begging for attention. One is the voice of the hurt child; the other is that of the critical parent. They seem to be adult in nature—we are adults, after all. But on careful inspection, we see that both the voices actually come from one desperate child within. This child causes us to go into autopilot and make unconscious choices. The result is that we live life by default rather than with awareness and by choice. It is important to know when our lives are being led by "the baggage" because without awareness, change cannot occur.

The Hurt Child

When you are being led by your hurt-child voice/state of being, the following behaviors can occur:

- You have the "disease-to-please"; you're obsessed about pleasing others so they will like you.

- You withdraw emotionally from others without letting them know why.
- You are rebellious and throw temper tantrums; this is actually the hurt teenager stage!
- You feel you are the victim, always saying, "Why me?" and, "Poor me."
- You live in fear, always in a panic, and you do not have trust or faith in life.
- You manipulate others emotionally, "guilting" them into doing something for you.
- You take people hostage with emotional blackmail.
- You fall apart so someone will take care of you.
- You are self-loathing and have low self-esteem, often because you experienced a lot of criticism growing up.
- You are always feeling attacked and are on the defensive.
- You don't take responsibility for your own life, and you blame others for things that go wrong.
- You feel that you are "not enough" and you "don't get enough."
- You focus on the past and live in regret.
- You aren't able to set clear boundaries; you allow others to invade your space.
- You feel that "life is unfair."

When any one of these traits is active or motivating your responses to life, it usually means that the hurt child is running the show; in other words, a four- or five-year-old child is running your life! The outcome often means poor decisions, reckless behavior, rifts in relationships, projections onto other people and general low self-esteem.

The critical-parent voice/state of being, on the other hand, seems very mature, very adult-like, but, in reality, the critical parent is the inferiority complex (the hurt kid) disguised in a superiority-complex outfit.

The Critical Parent

When your critical-parent voice/state of being is running the show, the following behavior can occur:

- You are judgmental.
- You are inflexible: "My way or the highway."
- Everyone walks on eggshells around you.
- You focus on "coulda, shoulda, woulda" and are often self-critical of the choices you make, and you are critical of other people's choices.
- You are ruled by the past, but you live in the future, aka "future worrying!"
- You behave in a passive-aggressive manner.
- You shame or blame others to manipulate them emotionally into doing things your way.
- You are an overfunctioner who takes on the roles of caretaker and enabler to control others and life in general.
- You are fearful and have no trust or faith in life.
- You are a perfectionist, and you are intolerant of others.
- You take people hostage with emotional blackmail.
- You are bitter and ungrateful.
- You appear to have a huge ego, but, in fact, you have low self-esteem.
- You have high expectations for others.
- You have no respect for boundaries; you invade others' boundaries.
- You behave and feel self-righteous.

We all, in fact, have at one time or another embodied the hurt-child and the critical-parent voices; we are flawed works in progress. Changing these dysfunctional states of being that create unhappiness requires profound awareness, willingness and courage to change so that these behaviors can be processed and neutralized.

It is important to know that when you take on the hurt-child voice, you attract the critical-parent voice/archetype like a magnet into your life, and vice versa. Where there is a damsel in distress, there is a knight in shining armor who rescues or the ogre who abuses. Real-life examples of the hurt child and the critical parent enmeshed in one another's lives include the person looking to be saved by a parental figure.

Look around and you will see this dynamic in action in various relationships: one "parentifying" the other, and another infantilizing the other; each state of being feeding on the other.

The only way to break the symbiotic loop of this dysfunctional dynamic, and thus create change in your life, is to seek with deep focus and intention to shift the behavior. As Maya Angelou said, "When you know better, you do better." If you are aware, you can break the loop, and the learning can begin sooner rather than later. When you move from blindly repeating your behavior, you can move toward neutralizing the pattern.

The Hurt Child Played Out in Adult Life: More Awareness

Whenever you are having difficulty in adult relationships, it is often because one or both people are coming from the hurt-child perspective. As the hurt child, you always want approval and to be loved, and you are oversensitive to criticism. You are also willing to be a chameleon who transforms yourself into whatever is necessary to get this approval and love and have a sense of belonging.

The overcritical home environment will bring about the need to be hyperintuitive and hypervigilant around other people and constantly wondering what others are thinking and feeling. The tentacles are out, "feeling" the situation, sensing the danger to find out if it is okay to proceed, and there is a lack of spontaneity as well. This can be extremely exhausting, and yet those who do it are largely unaware of their pattern of behavior.

Because this behavior was learned early in life, there is no logic behind it; often it developed in the preverbal months of children's lives. The children's authentic selves were stunted, even thwarted, as they became preoccupied with losing love and gaining a sense of belonging. They become so outwardly focused, seeking approval and acknowledgment, that they don't develop any spontaneity. They constantly ask questions such as "Do others love me?" "Am I accepted here?" and "What do I need to do to belong?" This chips away at their authentic selves.

As adults, this behavior continues, and their adult relationships repeat the pattern of being so out of touch with their authentic selves that they do not know their own limits and boundaries; thus, they constantly put themselves in situations that allow their core beings to be violated. As a result, they feel deeply betrayed. This often turns into resentment and evolves into manipulative, overreactive behavior that leads to much conflict in their relationships.

Never having been taught that love is unconditional and available to them at all times, they cannot relax and just be themselves. Their inner child's sense of "okayness" and their self-esteem rise and fall according to how they feel they are being perceived or treated. Children tend to test their limits, looking back to see if their parents are still with them as they do so. If the parents are harshly critical, the children will metabolize the criticism, and to get love and feel they belong, they will turn themselves into whatever is necessary to feel heard, seen and loved by the only group they know—their family and, specifically, their parents. In many cases, they will stifle their self-expression to achieve this.

When parents are caught up with their own problems, such as money, work, stress, addiction, depression and relationships, the children learn quickly that they aren't front and center in the parents' minds. They will often metabolize this as "I am not a priority" or "I am not important." It is important to note that this is not to blame parents; they have a tough job for which they are not formally trained, so they often just repeat what they have been shown. However, it is crucial in therapy to acknowledge the source of the patterns that show up in adulthood that compromise a person's happiness in life.

Projecting Old Family Dynamics at the Office

Workplace conflicts are extremely common and affect the bottom lines of companies. People complain that their bosses do not acknowledge them enough or they can't work with a difficult colleague. The common denominator that I see is that those involved may not be fully in their adult state. They are projecting their family dynamics onto their work environment and repetitively playing out their family-of-origin issues. This damages their ability to thrive and be successful at their jobs.

One example of this was Ben, who consistently felt that his boss took advantage of him and didn't acknowledge him. He always felt resentful toward his boss and poised for conflict with him. Yet, when I encouraged him to draw clearer boundaries, he felt he wouldn't be able to. He felt he was underpaid and overworked, but he was paralyzed when it came to asking for more money.

Unknowingly, Ben had been projecting his own issues with his father onto his boss. He had grown up with an absentee father who had given him very little attention and criticized him. In therapy, we learned that Ben was deeply afraid of rejection and abandonment by his father. As a result, he developed a pattern of not being able to speak his truth with male authority figures. Speaking authentically was simply not an option for a boy who just wanted to be loved and approved of by his distant, critical dad. In a skewed way, his boss had become a father figure to him. This unresolved family dynamic was playing itself out, and Ben was operating from his "hurt child" in his adult work environment.

Ben needed to become aware of this "father projection" to step into his "adult" at work. Once he was able to observe and understand what he was doing, he could see his boss more as a company man looking out for the bottom line of the corporation and not as a rejecting father figure. The only way Ben was going to get the kind of acknowledgment he craved was to first feel within like a valuable person who did not depend on an external authority figure for approval. This awareness propelled him to ask for more money and to successfully draw clearer boundaries in more fearless ways.

Becoming aware of what is actually going on when you are having conflicts at work is paramount to begin reversing the patterns. Is sibling rivalry at play with a colleague? Are you fighting to be heard and seen by a mother or father figure at work? Are you afraid to draw clear boundaries because you fear rejection? Are you operating from your hurt child or are you a balanced adult? These are questions to ask yourself so that you can reverse old self-sabotaging patterns that no longer serve you in your adult work life. Awareness is the key. Action based on that awareness is the answer.

Once you become aware of the patterns at play, you can begin to slowly change your reactivity in the workplace by telling yourself the real story: "These people are not my family!" You need to tell yourself that you cannot have the same expectations of the person you are dealing with at work as you would with a family member. You need to step into your "work self," which is your "adult self" and not your hurt or neglected "child self." With this understanding, you can compartmentalize any inappropriate emotions that arise at work. For example, if you feel rejected, jealous or abandoned because a co-worker, who seems to be the boss's pet, is snubbing you, check to see if you are playing out the family-culture dynamics you experienced at home growing up. Use logic to change your perspective. Regard your work life and the emotions you experience there as very different from anything personal. Whether you are self-employed or working for a company, know that the bottom line rather than emotional safety is the focus, and, as such, your work life has to have different boundaries and expectations.

Case Study: Breaking Free of the Hurt Child

John, who was extremely dissatisfied in his relationships, constantly felt betrayed and hurt. When he gave of himself to someone else, he expected a specific kind of reaction, which made his relationships very conditional. He was unconsciously preoccupied with the idea that the other person was going to react in a way that would trigger his insecurities and neediness. Inevitably, the person didn't step up to the plate of his expectations. Other people never measured up to his rigid preconceived idea of what they should do, say or feel. John controlled his world, and it became very small. He had a very judgmental, almost arrogant, disconnected way about him, which served as a protective plate for his deeply hurt and abandoned child within. He complained bitterly that when he gave to others, they weren't humble or grateful enough, and that they didn't do anything that he expected them to do. In his relationships with women, this just confirmed his belief that women always did this to him and he never got what he needed from them. In turn, this became an excuse for him to exit and amputate the relationship, which, in fact, he often did. At the same time, he suffered from a deep loneliness and wanted to have a healthy relationship with a woman.

During therapy, we discovered that he was harshly criticized and judged by his mother, and he felt a deep resentment toward her that he had never really got over, even though she was dead. John had never felt it was safe enough to be his authentic self with his mother. In a bid to resolve his hurt-child relationship with his mother, we discovered that he was unconsciously attracting into his life women with whom he felt unloved, unappreciated and unable to be authentic. As the therapy progressed, he began to discover his own part in this dynamic. He realized that he was constantly judging other people, and they would feel that they couldn't be themselves with him. It was a big aha! moment for him when he recognized the deep pain of the cruel criticism he had experienced as a child, and that he had been unaware that he was repeating this very behavior in his relationships. Ultimately, he understood that he had been acting this way to block intimacy and, thus, stay safe. He allowed only a small, safe window of reactions from his girlfriends so he would feel safe. His choices were based on his comfort zone, so he never truly allowed any relationship to flourish with all of its ups, downs, ebbs, flows and risks. He was after strict control and, therefore, predictable safety. He was keenly hypervigilant to any sign of rejection or judgment. Through therapy, John discovered that no real growth was possible and no real relationship could flourish in such a narrow, inflexible environment. These discoveries were deeply painful for this man, who had invested years in not feeling his true feelings by masking them with a strong outer layer of blind arrogance. He had been numbed, and thus doomed to repeating these unhealthy dynamics over and over again. In the end, the deep pain of his new awareness eventually became his freedom ticket. His awareness brought him the opportunity to make new and healthier decisions regarding the relationships in his life.

It is common to be in deep emotional pain, and yet completely numb to the pain. While in therapy, it can seem to some that the pain has increased; however, it is really the awareness that has increased, so one is then able to feel the pain that had been there all along. This is when the real healing starts. This is when the light at the end of the tunnel comes into view. But in order to get to the light, the person has to go through the tunnel, and that tunnel can be very dark and painful indeed. Facing one's dark side is a hero's journey, to be sure! But there is no way around it to get to the good stuff of life.

As I said earlier, sometimes I wish people the gift of despair. You might think I am cruel to say this, but why do I call it a gift? Because you can go on denying your authentic self, amputating those who don't give you what you want, being attracted to victims, basing your self-esteem on your perceived opinions of others, manipulating people and more. This hurt-child activity can continue ad nauseam when people remain numb. But their lives are not joyous. Despair is the wake-up call that I wish upon anyone going about life in this way because it gets them to a place of willingness to do whatever it takes to get back to "right thinking," back to their real selves.

You can try to avoid the pain and continue to ignore its life messages, but the hurt-child behavior keeps you from your true purpose on the planet: to be authentic and to find your self-culture. You need to go through the pain of awakening your authentic self; however, it is a good pain. It is a healing pain, like the pain of giving birth. Inevitably, when you begin to feel your authentic self for the first time, you will suffer a great deal because you are losing the trappings of your hurt child and the inauthentic life you had hidden from yourself to seemingly stay safe. The disease-to-please, the need to manipulate to have love, the need to control to maintain the status quo, the self-neglect to have the energy to take care of others, the enmeshing with other people's feelings to feel accepted—all these hurt-child behaviors are stripped away, leaving you feeling naked at first. In effect, you are creating a new paradigm for your state of being, and you have to deal with your true self. You are in the void, and since nature abhors a void, eventually, you will begin to fill this void with new ways of being, new tools. In this new paradigm, you no longer manipulate to get what you want; instead, you ask for what you want. You no longer shame yourself and others; you honor yourself and others. You are no longer helpless, passive or powerless; you bravely take action and confront life. You no longer lie and deceive to be seen in a better light; you risk displeasing others; you risk losing people if they are not appropriate for your self-culture journey. You no longer go deeply into debt, recklessly spending what you do not have; instead, you responsibly budget and sensibly assess your finances.

You step into your authentic adult self. You begin to see life from the adult perspective rather than the child perspective.

Please do the "Exercise for Developing Your Self-Culture" in appendix III often, and then begin to create new neural pathways with the "Exercise for Anchoring New Neural Pathways" in appendix IV.

Remember, awareness + willingness + courage = change. Once the three elements are in place, you can unearth the state of being of the "balanced adult voice." Once unearthed by calling deeply upon it, this innate state of being cannot be altered.

The Balanced Adult

How do you know when you are in your balanced-adult voice/state of being? When the following elements are in place:

- You are nonjudgmental.
- You allow others to be themselves.
- You are accepting of what is.
- You focus on and are oriented toward the present day.
- You have trust and faith in the process of life.
- You deal with adversity by seeing the larger picture; you ask, "What is the lesson for me here?" (I call this "transcendence thinking.")
- You take responsibility for yourself in all aspects.
- You draw clear boundaries and stick to them.
- You commit to not enabling the hurt child or the critical parent in yourself or others.
- You are compassionate, yet not a caretaker.
- You encourage others to care for themselves.
- You quiet your mind often and listen to your own divine guidance.

- You honor yourself and listen to your own needs.
- You are authentic.
- You have focused, clear, laser-beam intentions in life.
- You have a positive, buoyant attitude.
- You are oriented toward action rather than reaction.
- You believe that life is supportive.
- You are grateful.

Stepping into your empowered adult voice does not happen overnight. It is a process that evolves from a deep, repetitive practice of calling forward your balanced adult voice. The first steps begin with parenting yourself in compassionate ways. You begin to feel safe, which, in turn, encourages your authentic self to blossom. This is the way for the child to stop wanting to control and run the show. The child is set free and gets to relax as the balanced adult steps up to manage the store. The critical-parent voice also slowly tends to retreat once it feels there is some order and it is not being threatened.

This is a golden process that allows us to move beyond the elements that limit our growth. It brings us into healthy relationships with other people and allows us the opportunity to step into our greatness and into our authentic self-culture.

Chapter Eight

THE BULLY VERSUS THE COACH

To attain selfhood and achieve your goals, you need to be gentle with yourself. Often we think that if we can just be disciplined and strict enough with ourselves, we will be more successful. If we don't seem to be getting anywhere, we become impatient and get mad at ourselves, berating, criticizing, judging and yelling at ourselves. Do more! Be more! Go, go, go!

Our intentions are good; we want to be better people and fulfill our potentials, but this kind of self-talk can only cause us to shut down and rebel because it is abusive and devoid of love. It sabotages us and we lose our motivation. Deep inside our being, we hear the discipline without love and we perceive it as abuse.

The bully in us may be familiar because we have normalized it as a way to motivate ourselves; however, it is rarely effective, at least not for long. In fact, bullying ourselves has the opposite effect. If, for example, you set yourself a New Year's resolution, and then try to achieve it in a militaristic, punishing and rigid manner, you are bound to fail. Why is this? It is because your inner child begins to feel afraid, and so it rebels when you try to move away from your comfort zone. Your inner child says, "I'm afraid of change." "I feel lost." "It feels as though you're punishing me." Your inner child is screaming to be heard; it wants you to know that it wants to do better, but it wants to be comfortable in this pursuit. For example, if you want to improve your diet, and you shock yourself into a massive new eating regime that you force upon yourself, your system will respond by making you feel profoundly deprived. As a result, you may try to comfort yourself by binge eating, and your entire resolution will go down the drain.

To create a new pattern of behavior, you need to transform the bully voice within you into a supportive coach voice that will ease you gently into the desired change. In reality, the bully is *trying* to make you a better you, but in a misdirected way. To transform your inner bully, you need to speak to it as you would to a child who is frightened and throwing a tantrum. If you yell at the bully, it will simply yell back more loudly. To make a connection, you need to speak gently to it.

Visualization to Transform Your Inner Bully into a Supportive Coach

Sit in a calm space and close your eyes. Imagine yourself in a peaceful, natural setting. Call forth the bully in you; for example, you could imagine in detail a schoolyard bully. In your mind's eye, invite the bully to sit down with you. Be prepared to be open and nonjudgmental as you begin to ask the bully the following key questions and wait patiently for the responses.

1. What are you trying to do for me?
2. What is your positive purpose in my life?
3. What do you seek to accomplish by constantly being in my life?

The more open you are, the more information you will gather, and the more likely you will be able to neutralize and, ultimately, transform your destructive inner bully. If you listen carefully, the bully will tell you that it is trying to make you a better person.[1] It is trying to protect you from failure and disappointment. It is trying to encourage you to be the best you can be. However, as you know, it is failing miserably at this task because of its abusive tone.

Once you have heard the answers to your questions, you can tell the bully that you understand what it is trying to do for you. Tell the bully that its method is not effective. Thank the bully for its efforts, but that a new way is needed now.

It is important that you understand that this is a process of befriending your darker side; that is, integrating it into your whole being so that it knows that you are finally listening carefully to its underlying positive message, and that it will not have to yell as loudly at you to be heard. This type of dialogue is the way to transform the bully within yourself.

Continue to slowly visualize the bully becoming a more positive version of itself—a supportive and encouraging coach. Imagine this inner coach in detail, allowing its gentle, encouraging—yet strong —voice to emerge. Your coach might say to you, "I believe in you," "You are precious and lovable, and you deserve gentleness as you ease into your transitions," "Bit by bit you are getting to your goal" and "Consistency is the key to your success. Stick with it. I know you can do it."

1 This concept is based on one of the key principles of neuro-linguistic programming (NLP), "positive intention," which states that at some level of consciousness, all behavior is or was positively intended; that is, negative behavior is rooted in a positive purpose.

The coach within you will encourage you to try the 80/20 rule: 80% of the time, move in your desired new direction, such as standing up for yourself, being authentic, eating well, spending wisely or exercising, but do it gently, lovingly and kindly! Don't be too punishing! For the other 20% of the time, you may slip back to your old ways, but all the while you know that you are slowly improving. Tell yourself that every day you are getting better and better. Remember, slow change is permanent change. Be kind to yourself. Remember that your inner child needs gentle dialogue so it can get on board and stop sabotaging the adult who's trying to make positive life changes. (You will find the above visualization exercise repeated in appendix V.)

Case Study: If You Don't Tend to the Bully, the Rebel Shows Up!
Ryan came to see me because he thought he should be accomplishing more in his life, but he felt he was too lazy and not focused enough. He wanted some coaching to become a "doer." He did not realize that it was his bully that was troubling him.

In his therapy sessions, Ryan's unrelenting pattern of overachieving, along with a heavy dose of perfectionism, began to unfold. As a result of this pattern, he always felt that whatever he did was never enough. He was not enough. He did not earn enough. He was lazy. His wife was not enough—and he was in the middle of a divorce. In the case of his marriage, he had chosen a woman who was the mirror image of his inner bully. She was an ambitious woman, and she bullied him.

When we don't consciously resolve our darker sides, those characteristics will be mirrored in the partners, friends and associates we choose. However, these people can present us with opportunities to become aware of the patterns we need to resolve.

Once resolved, their power is neutralized, and we aren't doomed to keep repeating them.

I facilitated a process of closed-eyes, slow, deep introspection, in which we discovered Ryan's pattern of needing to be the doer of his family. He always tried to be the perfect son in his family of origin so that he could show up his sister, who was the eternal darling in his dad's eyes. He performed as the good son so perfectly that he enrolled only in school activities that would please his father, completely ignoring what he really wanted to take part in. And since these activities were so far from his natural tendencies, he had to push himself brutally to be good at them. Only through bullying himself did he manage to persist and succeed in volleyball and chess, which he couldn't stand. He would much rather have been involved in theater or music; however, his larger agenda was to be a success in his father's eyes.

As Ryan grew into adulthood, this patterning continued with the career choices he made. He bullied himself harshly to make it through business school, and he persisted through a career as an entrepreneur. By the time he was middle-aged, he found himself just wanting to escape on his motorbike. Finally, the rebel in him had shown up just in time to put the bully in its place. He longed to be on the open highway, where there was less pressure and he would be free. He longed to smoke and drink to escape his present reality. He went from bully to rebel when the pressure he had put on himself became too much, and he would take off on his motorbike and stay away for days at a time. However, when he returned to his real life, he was faced with the mountains of work that he had neglected, and he went back to bullying himself, feeling guilty for his escapist rebel tendencies. He hunkered down, and, inevitably, with the pace he sustained, he ended up physically debilitated and with a compromised immune system. He would become ill, which would temporarily shut down his inner bully and rebellion, but they would appear again, and he would repeat the cycle over and over again. When he first came to see me, he had recently had a bout of the flu that had lasted for months.

The only way Ryan would be able to heal this cycle was to allow his authentic self to show up. Only then would his bully/rebel dysfunction cease. Through therapy with visualization exercises and bodywork, Ryan was able to wake up his dormant inner coach. This more gentle side of him allowed for a freer exploratory dialogue to occur, which revealed that for Ryan to be successful without being driven to escapism, he needed to slow his pace down considerably.

Ryan balked at this truth; he didn't want to slow down. "Only losers have to go slower," he protested. "Why can't I do more? What is wrong with me?" I asked him to give it a try for a week. I gave him some homeplay to do—we worked out a simple schedule for the week that included a healthy combination of rest, work, play, exercise, socializing and meditation. He looked at our list and arrogantly judged it to be boring. "Of course," I said. "Ryan, you are used to the drama of the bully/rebel/collapse cycle. This is much tamer, but you came in here looking to be more productive. With this healthier way of being, you will achieve that in time."

He agreed to follow my suggestions and kept them up, and with each visit to the office, he was feeling stronger and less burdened by the relentless bully/rebel pattern. Periodically, he would ramp up the "doing," only to land up sick in bed. It took him months to fine-tune the balancing act and know what truly worked for him. Eventually, he found he could sustain only self-culture–oriented activities. Having tasted this, as soon as he went off the rails, his system would quickly nudge him back to his true self.

Chapter Nine

GETTING IN "RIGHT" RELATIONSHIP WITH SELF AND LIFE

You cannot have a good relationship with life if your relationship with yourself is off the rails. Developing a "right" relationship with yourself requires discipline in your way of thinking and a willingness to be in a teachable state of being with life. When living by these principles, a deep "rightness" with self and life will develop.

Here is your "toolbox," which contains six guiding fundamentals for you to work on to improve your "rightness" with yourself:

1. Watch Your Negative Running Commentary!

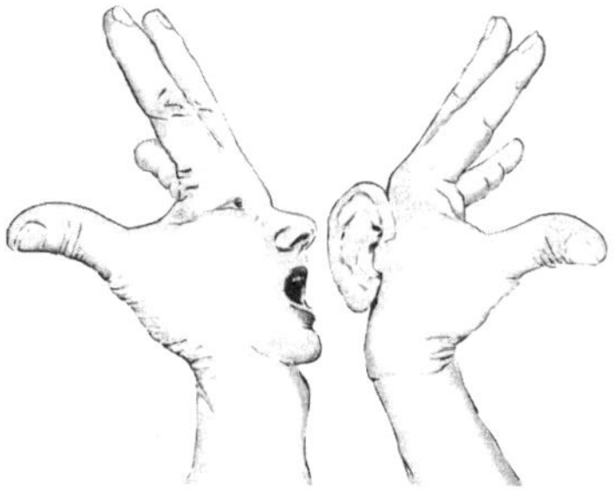

What are you saying to yourself?

Regularly bring your awareness to your mind's running commentary and watch what you are saying to yourself. We tend to be on autopilot most of the time, and yet our thoughts influence our vibration and state of mind, and because of this, our lack of awareness is like a vortex that is so engulfing that we do not even know its impact. We are like the frog that was placed in cold water and then slowly boiled to death, unaware that it was in danger. Like the frog, we don't even notice the destructive and, ultimately, deadly effects of our dysfunctional thinking because we have normalized it. We need to step out of the vortex of our unconscious negative running commentary to become aware of how it affects us.

It is widely understood that thoughts alter your vibrational frequency, which is measured in megahertz, and positive thinking raises your vibration, whereas negative thinking lowers it. We also know the Law of Attraction, which states that "like attracts like." Thus, your vibrational frequency determines what you attract toward yourself. If your running commentary is oriented toward worst-case scenarios, you will be more likely to attract negative events and states of being.

Catching yourself in a negative running commentary is so important; what I often tell my clients to do when they catch themselves, and what I do myself, is to stop everything! Ask yourself if you are **h**ungry, **a**ngry, **l**onely and/or **t**ired (HALT).[1] Being in any one or a combination of those states requires you to HALT and immediately make yourself a priority, no matter what else is going on.

You may indeed be in a situation that is painful, embittering, unfair or angering, and the truth is, you may have very little control over outcomes. However, what you do have control over are your thoughts and your attitude. You may need to fake it until you make it. Starting to take baby steps out of the vortex of negativity by uttering positive statements is a good beginning. Here are some examples:

1 The acronym HALT is a recovery tool used in 12-step programs.

- "The universe is conspiring on my behalf." (This is a great one to do over and over when you are not feeling inspired by anything.)
- "Everything is working out better than I expected." (This is one of my personal faves; it takes care of any negative expectations!)
- "All is well" and "I am safe." (These two simple statements are glorious affirmations to meditate on and visualize. Even just saying, "All is well" repeatedly like a mantra helps neutralize that negative running commentary, and it will reduce anxiety as well.)

Affirmations are so important because they are a way to keep the busy, negative, repetitive and primitive "monkey brain" of ours focused on the notion that there are limitless possibilities in any given situation. Instead of the black and white, concretized thinking, with affirmations, you are able to focus on the gray, which is more open-minded. Repeat them often, especially when you are challenging yourself or when you are afraid of a situation you are in. In this way, your mind will have something positive to attach to instead of to the negative fearmonger within.

Gratitude is so important also. Going as quickly as you can into gratitude, even in a negative situation, is a good discipline to practice. Being grateful during a negative situation for anything, even for being alive, able to breathe or able to talk can shift everything. You may find that your entire thinking shifts quickly as soon as you go into the vibration of gratitude.

Know that what you focus on expands. If you think of yourself as a victim, then the Law of Attraction principle will simply give you more of that. The universe does not punish or reward. If that were the case, all the good people would be wealthy and happy, and all the bad people would be miserable and poor. Look around, this is not the way it is. Instead, people bring toward themselves everything they focus on in the deep recesses of their repetitive thoughts, and as if the universe were a perfect mirror, they simply bring to themselves what they most often think about. This is supremely powerful knowledge to have. Use it to change your life!

Get busy and clear your mind of toxic waste, such as bitter and negative thoughts and thinking of yourself as a victim. Instead, infuse positivity into your brain cells, even if you aren't feeling positive! Be disciplined in this practice.

The situation you are in may not be resolvable, and if it is, it may not end any time soon. However, you do need to acknowledge the dark feelings, such as fear, hurt and anger, but give yourself a time limit. For example, give yourself a time frame of thirty minutes to one hour to indulge the negativity and deeply acknowledge the fear, sadness, hurt and anger. Cry and yell, and then write about it or share it with a trusted person. Naming the feelings and really feeling and honoring them have a remarkable way of dissipating the intensity. Once you have done this, with focus, take a baby step out of the muck and the mire. The difference now is that all of the darkness is no longer residing in your unconscious realm. It was the unawareness that was doing the damage and prolonging the agony.

Take care of yourself as you would a hurt child whom you love very much. Tending to your needs is a healing experience that will get you "right" with yourself, which, in turn, will quickly get you "right" with the world.

2. Mental and Emotional, Spiritual and Physical Fitness

Mental and emotional fitness, spiritual fitness and physical fitness form a trifecta of fitness that is necessary to getting in "right" relationship with yourself and your life, and it cannot happen if you don't work at it.

2a. Mental and Emotional Fitness

Mental and emotional fitness comes from a variety of ways of constantly caring for and nurturing yourself, and it is essential if you are to take on the more challenging aspect of seeking your own self-culture. A person can move through the fire in this process, but only if an environment that supports change is in place. Following are ways to increase your mental and emotional fitness:

- **Work consistently on being kind to yourself.** Always look for opportunities to affirm yourself—not in an arrogant way, but in a self-loving way. Be compassionate with yourself.
- **Speak nicely to yourself.** Speak to yourself as you would speak to your pet, your friend or your plant!
- **Don't engage in emotionally reckless behavior:**
    - Don't gossip, cheat, lie or engage in addictive behavior.
    - Don't take on more that you can handle.
    - Know your limitations.
    - Be discerning about whom you let into your intimate world.
    - Don't shame others or yourself.
- **Do the "Self-Comforting Hugging Exercise" in appendix VI often!** This "hugging yourself" experience is an opportunity for you to spend time acknowledging your feelings, which is a first step toward neutralizing them. This exercise is especially helpful when you move out of your comfort zone and

feel overwhelmed. Use it often as a means to relax any anxiety, self-doubt and nervous feelings.

- **Engage in a therapy**. This is so important when you are moving beyond your family culture. You can know something intellectually, but the journey from the head to the heart is the longest and most profound one. It is important to have a safe place to process the raw feelings. The reality is that you will often feel scared, crazy and wrong for carving a path to self-culture. A therapist is an amazing support for that profound journey. In therapy, you will be able to work on the areas of fear, self-doubt and any emotional conflict that may arise out of your moving into your self-culture.
- **Read inspiring books**. This was essential for me, and it is also very important for my clients. I can safely say that reading *You Can Heal Your Life* and *The Power Is within You* by Louise Hay woke me up with a bang over twenty-five years ago, and I have never looked back. There are also so many more books out there that can inspire you to move beyond where you are now. Please check out the selected bibliography at the back of the book for more ideas.
- **Hang out with cheerleaders rather than detractors**. This is so important! As you move beyond the familiar, it is paramount that you look around your life and see what is there. Are the people in your life going to support your movement toward selfhood, or are they going to keep you where they want you? This journey is not necessarily going to be easy. You need to make sure you have people around you who are in favor of and support your movement toward authenticity and selfhood.

2b. Spiritual Fitness

- **Be disciplined around meditation**. Meditate often and visualize yourself living your self-culture. This will calm your nervous system as you transform. Meditation will also give you the space to finally listen to your authentic voice within. It helps you to mentally focus. It helps to clear up the clutter of life. It helps to give you perspective so you can get through life's difficulties. Studies show that when you are in a relaxed state rather than the fight-or-flight mode, your immune system is actually stronger,[2] so you are able to more easily fight off some of the bugs that you might come into contact with. Meditation is also a very important skill to have to be able to clarify what you want to manifest in your life. Don't be too hard on yourself; try not to be a perfectionist. Gentle, gentle, gentle. Meditation is very important; I encourage you to practice it continually. There are many ways to meditate; these are a few of my favorites:
  - Walking outside just communing with nature is an act of meditation. Take in your surroundings while focusing on your breathing and the steps you are taking. Pay attention to the present moment.
  - Lie down comfortably and listen to a guided meditation—another voice taking you on a beautiful visual journey. I have created a guided meditation with beautiful music, which is available on my website at www.visualizationworks.com. This two-CD set is called *As Above, So Below*.

2 Suzanne C. Segerstrom and Gregory E. Miller, "Psychological Stress and the Human Immune System: A Meta-analytic Study of 30 Years of Inquiry," *Psychological Bulletin* 130, no. 4 (July 2004): 601–30, doi: 10.1037/0033-2909.130.4.601.

- I recommend a wonderful user-friendly book by Thomas Ashley-Farrand called *Healing Mantras: Using Sound Affirmations for Personal Power, Creativity, and Healing* for people to read to introduce themselves to doing mantra work. The phenomenal Sanskrit mantras in this book are incredibly transforming. You can also buy a strand of mala beads, which are meditation beads that help motivate you and help you keep track of how many mantras you do in a sitting.
- Train your mind as you would train a puppy: Be consistent, be disciplined, be loving.

2c. Physical Fitness

- **Eat well**. Regularly eating sugar promotes moodiness, anxiety and depression and can make you behave in a volatile manner. It is important to know how to eat in a way that does not affect your mind and emotions. Your body needs special treatment. That means very little sugar, caffeine and processed foods. Science shows us that the more your blood sugar is balanced, the more your emotions are balanced.[3] Yet deprivation is not the intention. If you feel you want to consume the occasional sweet treat, just make sure it is a high-quality treat. The darker the chocolate, the better. Fruit is also a more healthful alternative when you want something sweet, and there are so many varieties of fruit to choose from that help with sweet cravings. If you like coffee, try to keep your consumption down to one cup per day. After all, your body is precious, and you need to send it messages—on the mental, emotional, spiritual and physical levels—that you care and that you are committed to it.

3 Sue Penckofer et al., "Does Glycemic Variability Impact Mood and Quality of Life?" *Diabetes Technology & Therapeutics* 14, no. 4 (April 2012): 303–10.

- **Avoid that bloated feeling**. If you feel bloated after eating, it could be an indication that you have food sensitivities and allergies. Wheat, gluten and dairy are major culprits for many. Often when people are frequently bloated, an emotional feedback loop is set into motion. This is what I have observed: When people are feeling down, they eat comfort food that may contain dairy, sugar, wheat or other foods that they are sensitive to, as a result, they become bloated, and then they feel guilty and ashamed because they know they are not treating their bodies as they want to; this then leads to a lowering of their self-confidence, which, in turn, promotes feelings of self-doubt and self-loathing. If you experience this, try doing the "Dialogue with Self While Eating Exercise" in appendix VII; it will often mitigate this feedback loop.
- **Make time for rest and relaxation**. Try to keep a regular sleeping routine. When you live according to your circadian rhythm, your immune system will be stronger and you'll have more energy. Getting enough sleep at night also helps to tame anxiety and depression. If you have trouble with sleep, some natural sleep aids include chamomile tea; 3 mg of chewable melatonin taken fifteen minutes before bed; Calms Forte, a homeopathic remedy, taken before bed; using a sleep mask to block out light and/or ear plugs to block out sound; not using your electronic devices one hour before bed; not drinking caffeine past noon; and doing slow, deep breathing for fifteen minutes before bed.
- **Do yoga.** Yoga is amazing for keeping the body and the mind in tune and fit.

- **Work out and stretch.** Working out and doing stretching exercises are my personal favorites. T. Harv Eker wrote a book called *Secrets of the Millionaire Mind*, and in it he says, "How we do some things is how we do everything." If we treat our bodies well, chances are we will treat our minds, our spirits and others well too. Similarly, if we treat our bodies badly, chances are we will treat our minds, spirits and others badly as well. Getting regular exercise is essential for physical fitness, and it is key to feeling good about yourself, your mind and your life.
- **Try to get regular sessions of physical and energy therapy.** Polarity therapy, craniosacral therapy, massage, reiki, shiatsu and acupuncture are holistic modalities that are fantastic for energy balancing. Practitioners of these therapies are great sources of support, and the benefits are cumulative and far-reaching beyond the session. Try to find a holistic psychotherapist who combines mind and bodywork.

3. Future Worry Much? Past Obsess Much? Get into the Present Moment!

The present moment is where the meat of life is. This is where it all happens. And yet we seem to be obsessive about the future and the past. It is the dwelling on the past and worrying about the future that promotes the inner suffering.

Are you always waiting for the other shoe to drop? Do you worry obsessively about the future, even though things in the present are okay? Are you constantly basing your now on past situations? If so, realize that you may be drama-addicted. The stories you tell yourself about the unknown future, or about the dead past, may be horror stories you tell yourself. They occupy so much space in the present of your life, to the point where life is passing you by, without your being fully in it or, more to the point, without your learning from it. How can you learn from your life if you are not fully conscious of nuance and subtle messaging? It is all there for your growth, but you are missing it if the future and past are more important to you.

Getting into "right" relationship with yourself and with life requires that you focus on the present moment. Future worrying, that is, living as if something bad is going to happen, steers you away from the "right" relationship with yourself.

Remember that behind every negative pattern lies an unconscious positive motivation. Doing some introspective work can help you to neutralize your negative pattern and reveal your positive motivation. A way to do this would be to first slow your breath to calm yourself. Then ask yourself what might be your positive motivation behind your pattern of worrying about the future or dwelling in the past and not staying in the present moment. Wait for some clear ideas about this to arise. Here is a hint: A possible unconscious positive motivation could be that you are trying to gain control over your life because you are afraid of uncertainty. You want to feel safe. By focusing on the scary future, for example, you may think you are mitigating potentially being blindsided by failure or disappointment. You tell yourself to prepare for the worst so you can avoid feeling disappointed or caught off guard. In this way, you may think you have control over your life, and this is keeping you safe. It is true that life can be filled with unknowns, uncertainty and risks; therefore, your monkey brain tells you to be cynical so you don't get your hopes up.

When you are anxious, this seems like a reasonable way to conduct your life, and it may make you feel as though you have a measure of control and safety. However, in the long term it is destructive to your well-being and ability to be joyful. It is so far from the purpose you were put here for: to learn, grow and evolve. You become addicted to "safety" in a life that is narrow in scope and possibility. It negates your ability to accept that life is complicated and messy, yet filled with opportunity to evolve. The truth is, the other shoe may drop; bad things may happen. People may leave you. Life may not be perfect, but it is your life, and you can choose to live it well.

However, we cannot negate the positive purpose of having control and feeling safe, and we can attain this without obliterating living in the present. You can build some parameters into your life that create safety and give you a sense of control. Here are some examples of what you can do:

- Create routines for taking care of things such as your health, spending and work.
- Create an action plan that helps you accomplish your goals.
- Seek out mentors and support so you don't feel alone.
- Create community and fellowship in your life.
- Leave room for playtime and leisure.
- Commit to creating balance in your life.

These actions will give you the sense of control and safety that you seek, and, at the same time, they will keep you firmly rooted in the present. "Rightness" with self and life means getting into a deliberate relationship with your present moment.

4. Blame versus Responsibility: Know the Difference

> "The only thing blame does is to keep the focus off you when you are looking for external reasons to explain your unhappiness or frustration."
> — Wayne Dyer

When you are in "right" relationship with life and self, you are clear about the difference between blame and responsibility. They are on opposite sides of the spectrum. You may think that when you blame yourself for something you are taking responsibility for it, but you are not. In fact, you are doing the opposite. When you are "in blame," you are in a negative state; you are creating low self-esteem and engaging your bullying, shaming self. You lose all sense of self-value, and your ability to perceive the situation as a learning opportunity goes out the window. Instead, the situation becomes a punishment sentence. It is imprisonment versus rehabilitation. In addition, consider that being in continual self-blame encourages a state of depression.

On the other hand, when you take responsibility for something, you acknowledge that you have done something wrong, but you are in a proactive, positive state of being, looking to transform the situation. You are taking measures to correct whatever you have done. You are humble, open and positive. You see that nothing happens without a purpose. You own your part in a situation. Your "right" relationship mentality encourages you to be in a teachable state, which allows you to take negative experiences and transform them into life lessons.

5. We Teach People How to Treat Us

At every turn in a relationship, we teach people what is acceptable or not in our dealings with them. Being aware of the dynamics you allow with friends, partners, family, bosses and co-workers is extremely important.

So many people feel mistreated, victimized, berated and belittled by a variety of people in their lives. They are passed over for promotions, not paid back money they lend to people and they constantly feel they are being taken advantage of. I encourage everyone to analyze themselves and their relationships to see how they have essentially taught others—trained them—that it is okay to step on their toes, invade their boundaries and not treat them with respect.

One person I worked with was constantly complaining that he was not paid enough for what he did. People around him had been promoted or received raises and bonuses, and yet he remained in the same position with the same salary that he had had for the last five years, and he was petrified to ask for a raise. He had befriended his boss, so they were confidants, shall we say, and he didn't want to rock that relationship boat. He felt a misguided sense of loyalty, and my advice to him was to understand that this was business. I told him that there was a possibility that his boss knew perfectly well that he wasn't able to ask for a raise, and that it was to the boss's advantage to keep the status quo. This boss was not going to give him a raise of his own accord. My client needed to show the boss what his value was through asking to be compensated appropriately.

This is a common theme for many people. If you're in a relationship in which you feel you are being taken advantage of, or belittled or invaded, you need to take responsibility for having somehow trained the other person to treat you that way. You are not the victim, and you cannot blame someone else. Take back your power. Take back your strength and sense of self-loyalty and assert your boundaries. Tell people what is okay and what isn't. Advise people in a gentle, kind and loving way that it is not okay to treat you with disrespect or to belittle or humiliate you. If people are treating you this way, and you are not calling them on it, you need to analyze why you are unable to stand up to them and create the courage to tell them where you're at. I invite you to be brave and teach your friends and family, co-workers and bosses—and whomever—how to treat you appropriately. You have that right!

6. Compensating Childhood Behaviors: You May Not Need Them Anymore!

Carrying an old role from your family culture into adulthood can block you from living as your authentic self. It can stunt growth and overall joy. Your childhood behavior may have been useful to you to survive then, but today it can prevent you from living a full life.

Every family has its own dynamics that can cause children to engage in compensating behavior to survive emotionally, and then as adults they don't really experience true authenticity because they are still entrenched in childhood behaviors and roles that they unconsciously maintain, such as being the comedian, the chameleon, the pleaser, the troublemaker, the drama queen, the spender, the rebel, the baby. Ask yourself, "What compensating behavior from my childhood is still part of my personality and is no longer helping me in my life?"

Many of the compensating behaviors that you might have carried from your childhood into your adult life need to be modified. For example, if you are a comedian, keep your comedic timing and sense, but be discerning with what you keep and what you don't because, for instance, if you played the role of the pleaser, you may need to temper this behavior substantially so that you are not debilitated in relationships by always trying to please everyone to avoid the pain of being rejected or abandoned. Chameleons also need to watch for behavior in which they change their personalities, depending on the group they are with. They need to watch that they do not completely lose their identities to the point where they themselves and no one else really knows who they are.

Sit and meditate with the part of yourself that is playing the role that no longer serves you. Feel a sense of gratitude toward this part for having helped you survive your family dynamic. Acknowledge that you engaged in the behavior at a time that you had no say and no real power. But now you are an adult, and you have the power to live more authentically. You can choose to step out of the old behavior that you were pigeon-holed into and decide to live your true self-culture.

Chapter Ten

LISTENING TO THE HIDDEN MESSAGES IN NEGATIVE-PATTERN BEHAVIOR

You find yourself in the middle of a dissatisfying life. You consistently feel betrayed. You attract chaos to yourself and cannot figure out why. These pieces of you scream for attention and to be healed. The messages get louder and louder and show up as self-sabotage that reverberates at the speed of light into your relationships. One relationship after another doesn't work out. Your life lacks passion. You almost always feel bitter. The question is, how can you heal those pieces of yourself that are dark and most certainly poised to ruin your life for good if not addressed immediately? The ability to tap into the wisdom that lies within your life experiences is so crucial for your journey toward living your self-culture.

Any repetitive negative behavior is there for a good reason.[1] Your habitual pattern is trying to dialogue with you. It is trying to teach you something fundamental about yourself—something that you most probably are not even aware of. This behavior is an attempt to give you some sort of message that will benefit you, although it occurs in a very off-kilter way. We already know that most repetitive negative behavior started in childhood. We learned during this formative time that this behavior had a beneficial outcome, and we are convinced that it will continue to be of benefit

1 In neuro-linguistic programming (NLP), a negative behavior is understood to have a subconscious "positive intention," or positive purpose, in our lives.

now. What we learn very early tends to inform our perception for the long haul.

For example, you may have learned that a particular behavior could bring you some sort of emotional safety, protection, love or belonging within the family dynamic. It was the only way to survive and included emotional manipulation, playing the victim, criticizing, abusive yelling, withdrawing, clinging, falling apart so someone would rescue you, bullying, rebelling, being sarcastic, placating, people-pleasing and the list goes on. These are all negative behaviors that you may have used in order to survive, negotiate and even succeed through the minefield of a dysfunctional family. Tactics that once were effective in childhood will endure deep into adult relationships if left unchecked.

Case Study: Tiana

Tiana, who had worked diligently on herself, came to see me initially with habits and addictions that had more to do with relationships than with substances, yet were much more damaging to her life. Through the course of therapy, we discovered that she had a cavernous fear that she would lose love, approval and a sense of belonging and comfort if she expressed herself and lived authentically. She had no idea how to set clear boundaries with people. She regularly permitted people, friends, lovers and family members to take advantage of her financially, sexually and with her time. She was taught and shown as a child through her parents' behavior toward her that she literally had to be like a chameleon to get any kind of love, affection, attention or approval from them. She had to literally play a role within her family dynamic. She became extremely adept at ignoring her own values, needs and wants in favor of those of her parents.

Her mother was a perfectionist, and at times she was abusive to her when she became frustrated with her life. Tiana learned very quickly how to become whatever her mother wanted her to be, including her confidant. She learned to soften her mother by tending to her needs. At a very early age, she would regularly be privy to the very adult content of her mother's various affairs. Concurrently, her father was emotionally absent and a workaholic so that the only way she could get his attention was to learn to speak his business language, which she managed to do by the age of thirteen. However, this wore her down and led her to completely abandon her own interests and her own voice as she grew up. This was her survival tactic within her family dynamic, and later in her adult life as well.

As an adult, Tiana felt at the mercy of the men and the relationships in her life. She grieved her lost authentic self, which had gone down a rabbit hole, and she could not find her way back to it. Deep fear of rejection often compelled her to perform and to deceive. She engaged in many affairs, and she battled with bouts of explosive temper tantrums that made her feel even worse about herself. Yet, interestingly enough, therapy revealed that those tantrums were the only way her true self could make itself known. She had been ignoring all the other signs and messages that her core self had been trying to communicate to her. The tantrums finally made her listen. This, ironically, was a gift in disguise because it led to her wanting to understand herself for the first time.

What began to facilitate the healing of her old self-sabotaging behavior was feeling safe and empathized with. For the first time, she felt heard and seen. A compassionate environment provided the space where she dared to reveal some truthful fragments of herself. This was especially crucial for healing that deeply hurt and deprived child within. Therapy brought her that. We dialogued in depth about the fact that all human beings are deserving of love and compassion, no matter what they have done. We are not our actions. Taking responsibility for our actions does not mean we have to crucify ourselves forever.

As Tiana heard and metabolized this new perspective, deep healing began to permeate her being. She started to give herself permission to get in touch with who she was—her core self—before the performing had begun. She was so surprised that she could actually touch the edge of that part of herself.

Eventually, Tiana got that she had been behaving as she had been to stay safe, find love and belong. But she was just doing it all in a skewed fashion. She began to find some compassion for her hurt and deprived inner child as she realized all of this. This compassion for self is vital. When people sabotage themselves, abandon themselves, posture, cheat, lie, withdraw and engage in addictive behavior of all kinds, somewhere inside they are motivated by a need for safety, protection, love, belonging or some other positive outcome.

In our therapy sessions, I asked her, "What do you perceive to be the benefit of abandoning yourself in life and in your relationships? What is that negative behavior actually trying to do for you?"

No one had ever posed these questions to her. How could there be a benefit to such destructive behavior? But, in fact, she would not have engaged in any of the negative-pattern behaviors unless there had been a benefit. The true healing and metamorphosis that can happen within the therapeutic context comes from understanding this crucial notion. There is a perceived, often unconscious, benefit to negative behaviors. We must not throw the proverbial baby out with the bathwater. These negative behaviors are clues for us to examine. They are messages for us to listen to. Seeking love, safety and belonging is, in and of itself, a good impetus. However, the method to get to this positive state is what needs to be looked at and replaced with a healthy way of accomplishing this. We began to look for positive and healthy ways for Tiana to get what she needed. Step by step, she began her journey of making peace with her true self. This was not an easy process because she had no memories of feeling safe in being honest, clear or unguarded. New memories had to be created.

Her initial steps were simple but profoundly effective. She began for the first time to journal her feelings daily. This began to signal to her being that she was listening for the first time to her own voice. Wow, and what a voice! She discovered for the first time that she longed to explore yoga, photography and painting, all of which had eluded her in the past. She may have taken a class or two because her boyfriend was into art, but never because she had chosen it. It was so profound for me to witness this woman for the first time finding her own rhythm and her own sense of selfhood. Eventually, she left all of her destructive relationships behind. One by one, friends who once were there only to use her began to fall away from her life as she started drawing boundaries and saying no. The void in her life began to fill up with supportive friends and creativity as she recognized her worthiness. She started treating herself with respect and saying yes only to those things that she truly wanted to say yes to. A real metamorphosis had begun. She was filling her own needs for the first time in positive and healthy ways. Her sense of self-love, safety and belonging were happening without compromising her being.

If negative-pattern behaviors are present in adult life, it is vital to stop and really listen and learn from them as opposed to ignoring them. What are they trying to tell you? What are the perceived benefits to those behaviors? The patterns can start to subside and their loud messages will calm down if you just pay close attention to the dialogue they are trying to have with your core self.

Chapter Eleven

CATEGORIZING FRIENDSHIPS: PUT PEOPLE WHERE THEY BELONG

As you step deeper into your self-culture journey, how you relate in your various friendships will potentially change. It is important to have a methodology to work with as you assess these important relationships.

What draws us toward friends is usually a mystical chemistry that is brought on by mutual likes and dislikes, history, commonality of energy and a dash of simpatico dust for good measure. There is usually a wonderfully long honeymoon period between friends that lasts until the first conflict, at which point both parties will have to navigate the new landscape, and they will quickly learn how the other handles conflict.

Conflict can be handled, or not handled, in many ways. Is the way it is being dealt with healthy or not? Does one person stop talking to the other (I call that an "amputator") when they are angry? Does passive-aggressive behavior occur, in which sarcasm and jabs become the mainstay of the dialogue? Do the two just ignore the problem altogether, and then brace for a future explosion? No matter what the situation, friendships can be messy, disappointing and challenging. It is also true that we need friendships in our lives to have balance. Life is more expansive with friends than without. But we need to have a system that works if we want to experience our friendships in a healthy way.

Ask yourself this question: Are your expectations appropriate, or do you have expectations of a friend that you should not? If you do not ask this question, you are bound to be disappointed by your friends. You need to assess your friendships and see where you want to put them. It can help to know the level of friendship you are at with each friend. Please see the chart on the opposite page, which outlines three groups for friendships (A, B and C); one for people you are obliged to be in contact with (D); and others (E), who are not friends. Each group describes the kinds of expectations you would have from that group. It is important that you are mindful of which group you put your friends and acquaintances in. Following is a detailed description of each group.

Group A: These are your closest of friends—your life-and-death people. The people in your life with whom you are most intimate. You would have only one or two friends in this group, three if you're lucky. They are the friends who will be present for or participate in the important events and milestones in your life. They have earned this spot because of tried and true times together. They have never betrayed you, and vice versa. You feel safe revealing confidences to them, even your darkest thoughts, because they have shown themselves to be able to keep your private information confidential. You also respect and feel a love for one another. You are nonjudgmental with each other, and you are entirely safe to be your authentic selves with one another. Your expectations are higher than in any group, though they are realistic. You can count on these friends in life-or-death situations. They are the people you call upon if you are ill or some tragedy happens in your life.

Manage the People in Your Life

In which group do you place the people in your life?
What expectations do you have of each group?

GROUP A: This is the most intimate group. These are the people you can count on for life-or-death situations. You are lucky to have one or two friends from this group. You have mutually high expectations of one another.

GROUP B: These people are also close to you, but not as intimately as with those in group A. They include close co-workers, good social friends and good neighbors. You have lower expectations of one another than of those in group A, though your expectations are still quite high; however, you don't depend on them for life-or-death situations.

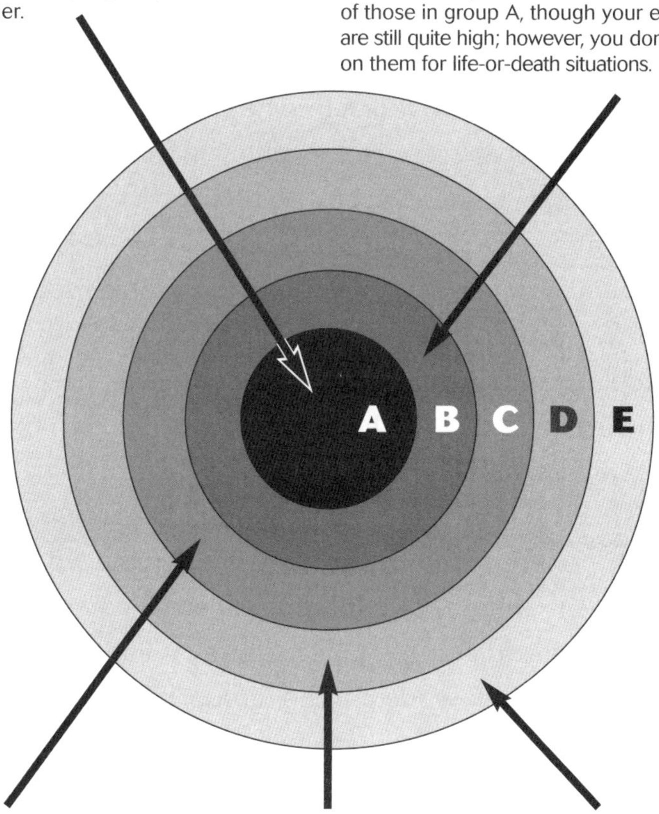

GROUP C: These people are acquaintances whom you like but are not sure yet if you are compatible. They can also be old friends who have been downgraded due to unpleasant experiences with them or repetitive dysfunctional patterns. You have low expectations of these people.

GROUP D: These are people you are not really fond of but with whom you are obliged to stay in contact. You have virtually no expectations of these people. You are courteous with them, but you are not friends. Examples may include your boss, your boss's spouse, co-workers, tenants, and some family members.

GROUP E: This is the group with whom you are the least close, and you have zero expectations of them. Examples include bank tellers and shopkeepers.

Group B: This group is probably larger than group A. You are quite close to these people, but not as close as you are to those in group A. They are also friends, but not as intimate as those in group A. You enjoy socializing with them, and you can be intimate with them, but you somehow feel that you need to be a bit more cautious with them as you have detected some problem patterns at times. These folks are people you adore, but you may have noticed some issues that make them perhaps less trustworthy or less emotionally safe to allow yourself to be fully vulnerable with. You need to observe what they are showing you through their actions and behavior, and you need to believe them so that you can adjust your expectations. Do not put people indiscriminately into your B group just because you have had some close times together. You also wouldn't put a person you have just met into this group. B-group people have been with you a long time, and they are fun to socialize with and share life experiences with, but they may not be good listeners, for example, or they may have a foible that prevents you from getting too close to them. If the foibles of a friend in this group continue to get worse, this is a sign that you may need to downgrade them to the next group. There is no need to amputate someone from your life unless there is real abuse; you just need to move them down to another group, where your expectations are lower and more in keeping with what you have learned from this person's actions. Also, I don't recommend doing business with B-group friends since the "business" agenda could change the dynamic, and you may end up having to downgrade the person to C group due to the shift in the relationship. Having your real estate agent as a friend, for example, requires that the friendship take a back seat to the business relationship. You may not be able to be as relaxed telling your agent what to do if they were a friend. This type of double relationship may not be smooth in this category.

Group C: These are our glorious acquaintances. Most of us have many of them in our lives. They include co-workers, downgraded B-group friends and friends of friends. You have very low expectations of these people from the friendship perspective. You could do business with C-group people since the friendship is not the priority. You see them occasionally socially, and you are happy to see them, but you do not go out of your way to connect with each other. These are the folks who, when they ask you, "How are you?" you answer, "Fine," no matter what you are really feeling. You don't reveal everything you are feeling; instead, you show them only the social you. It is unwise to be vulnerable with someone with whom you feel you cannot be emotionally safe.

Group D: These are people with whom you are obligated to be social, such as your boss, your boss's spouse, a neighbor, some co-workers or some family members. You don't particularly like them or have anything in common with them, and you have virtually no expectations of one another, but you are courteous with one another.

Group E: These are the people you might run into or need to do business with throughout your day, such as shopkeepers. You have zero expectations of these people.

I am not a fan of habitual amputation of friendship relationships that have disappointed you. If you were to amputate every person who let you down, there would be very few people left at the end of the road, and you would end up being isolated and your world smaller and smaller as you got older. Again, unless there is real and serious abuse, you would not amputate someone completely from any of your groups; however, relegating that person to another category, in which you adjust your expectations accordingly, is a more reasonable and less dramatic way to go.

Case Study: Categorizing Expectations in Relationships

Claire came to see me, wanting to know why her friends were always letting her down. She wanted them to be a certain way, and she couldn't stop feeling hurt by them. I detected that her expectations were off-kilter. Inappropriate expectations are usually the downfall of relationships, so it is important to place friends in the right group.

Claire told me the story of one of her old friends who consistently let her down, and how she saw a pattern where many of her friends disappointed her; she couldn't understand why she kept bringing that into her life. She was quite sad about it, and she was getting ready to amputate everyone so she could live an emotionally safer life, even though it would mean living a life with much fewer friends.

I explained to Claire that relationships, to be sure, can be messy, especially since we have friends and acquaintances in many different areas of our lives. I showed her how to group the people in her life so she could establish the appropriate expectations she could have for each one. When she used this tool, it was quite amazing to see how much happier and emotionally safer she felt. She became very clear about where to put her friends. For example, her "best" friend, who was constantly gossiping about her, betraying her trust and not showing up for dates they had made, was safely placed in her C group now. Claire's expectations of this friend became more appropriate. She had to grieve the loss of the dream of the friendship she thought they had, but she was able to make space to meet new people whom she could teach how to treat her.

She went about this systematic process of placing all the people in her life in their appropriate categories according to how they behaved and how she felt with them. Her expectations changed based on the group in which she placed the person. As a result, she felt more empowered and emotionally equipped to deal with relationships in general.

Chapter Twelve

MASTERING THE ART OF HEALTHY LOVE RELATIONSHIPS

Are You Behaving Like a Hostage?

What does a hostage do? A hostage will do whatever it takes to avoid danger and pain. Hostages will suppress everything they need and want in order to stay safe. The captor's needs and wants are far more important as there is a sense that they will continue to treat you reasonably well if you are devoted to their needs. When you behave like a hostage with another person, your self-love is very low and your relationship is profoundly codependent and unbalanced, and there are no boundaries. Relationships without good, clear boundaries will result in resentment and eventual destruction. The people involved end up doing things they really don't want to do and are largely unconscious of their actions.

This happens in love relationships where people are not empowered to behave authentically, and they put their own wants and needs on the back burner. Their insecurities are so strong that they do whatever it takes to avoid being abandoned by the other. This feeds the destruction of their self-esteem, and they end up abandoning themselves.

Hostage behavior usually begins in the family of origin during childhood when the person observes the family dynamic and how members of the family treat one another as well as people outside the family. People take cover as they experience violent communication, name-calling, invasion of boundaries, no privacy, overenmeshment and unsolicited advice being handed out freely—especially during the teen years, when the person was trying to individuate. Later, in adulthood, love relationships are imbalanced because the person has no sense of "I have value" and "I can really be authentic and true to myself." Watch for hostage and hostage-taking behavior in your love relationships. Become aware that this dynamic is not serving you in any way. Know that most healthy relationships are those that involve freedom of choice and expression.

Demanding Too Much Too Soon

Anna was with a man who really liked her, then one day he just stopped calling, started ignoring her calls and texts and told her, "You want too much too soon." She needed to consider that this man was perhaps an emotional withholder/abandoner, but even more importantly, she needed to see her own part in this dynamic. Following are three points that are very important when dating a new person:

1. **Impulsiveness is your enemy.** If you feel like calling or texting just because you are feeling lonely, don't! One call or one text is sufficient, and then let the other person come to you. Trust that they will, and if they don't, then perhaps you are not a match.
2. **Slow it down.** My philosophy is that for the first three months it is not a good idea to talk to each other every single day. I know that the initial excitement makes people want to see each other all the time, but for a healthy connection, it is important to not become overwhelmed with the other person. Try to keep it to no more than once or twice a week. Also, I suggest that

you not engage in sex for at least a month. I understand that each person has their own moral code, but it is my opinion that the longer you wait for sexual intimacy, the better chance you have of emotional intimacy evolving. Physical intimacy tends to overshadow everything else.

3. **Give each other space.** Have you ever heard the saying "Familiarity breeds contempt"? This is a valid maxim. The faster you become familiar with one another, the faster you're going to start nitpicking, criticizing and judging each other. So give one another time and space. And, of course, draw boundaries. Have a boundary for your personal activities. If you are trying to fill your life with the person you are dating, clearly your life is not full enough with your own sense of self. Ideally, when going into a new relationship, have a strong sense of self. Don't make the other person the center of your life—it never works. Remember, you are the main course in your life, and the person you are dating is the side order!

In Anna's case, she hadn't been truly listening to what her boyfriend was telling her about himself through his behavior. She needed to believe him when he was showing her who he was. If he wasn't calling her, it was best if she didn't call him. If he ignored her, it was a sign that he was not going to take care of her needs and that he was not good at communicating that he needed his space. No matter the reason, she needed to focus on her own life. Anna's childhood was fraught with emotional withholding and dysfunction. What she encountered growing up in her family culture led to her playing out this lack in her adult relationships. For example, if a daughter feels ignored by her dad, she is likely to attract this dynamic to herself and replay it with her partners. She projects her childhood needs onto them, and if this isn't resolved, it will turn into a desperate demand in her love relationships to get what she didn't get at home.

Anna had to understand that her boyfriend couldn't give her what she didn't get from her family of origin. I suggested that she back off, take it slower and give herself more personal space. In this way, Anna would give herself an opportunity to really see what was going on versus imposing her neediness on the relationship. This was the only way to see if her relationship would stand a better chance of being successful, healthy and happy. In the end, Anna and this boyfriend didn't make it, but she later met another man with whom she was able to set healthy boundaries and apply all she had learned from the first relationship. The awareness she gained from her therapy process also led her to make much better decisions, which led her to experience self-culture while still being in a relationship.

Setting Boundaries

Boundaries: Selfhood Savior!

Relationships without good, clear boundaries can result in resentment. And if self-esteem is also lacking, people can behave like hostages in their bid for love and not to be abandoned.

When does being generous become being a doormat? When does being a "can-do" person become a problem? These are questions that many contend with as they learn about setting healthy boundaries. By definition, a boundary is the line we draw between ourselves and others to protect our emotional and physical spaces. Setting proper boundaries is important to our mental, emotional, physical and professional health. When we don't set appropriate boundaries, we run the risk of becoming resentful, depressed, overwhelmed and inauthentic. When poor boundaries are in place in a relationship, the relationship becomes messy, and we can end up being too detached, overself-protective and isolated from others, or too dependent and overenmeshed with them.

We develop our worldview by the time we are six or seven years old, and our sense of self is impacted by that view. The messaging, relationships and ways of communicating in our families create that worldview and affect the way we are as adults. As children, we develop—or not—our self-esteem and learn whether or not boundaries are safe to have. A person may learn that a survival tactic in a family is not to have any boundaries in order to feel that they belong to and are loved by the tribe. They may learn that the only way to survive is to be compliant and abdicate all power, privacy and individuality. In these families, people are taught that it is rude to have boundaries; there is a lot of unsolicited advice, overprotectiveness and lack of privacy, and then, when it is more toxic, there is a lot of passive-aggressiveness, criticism and manipulation using guilt as a tactic.

The message is, "it is not polite or desirable to say no," or "be a good girl or boy and do whatever I say." In these cases, children are taught not to question the family culture because being an individual is considered a threat to the family's well-being. Those kids often end up being overly compliant and coercible at school and end up on the receiving end of bullying. Then, as they mature, the relationships they accept in their lives are imbalanced, and they often give more than they receive. They repeatedly allow their partners to be unfaithful to them and their friends to use them, and they are known for not ever stating their preferences.

Culturally, we find it difficult to say no. We are taught to be accommodating. Women particularly seem to struggle with empowering their "no" without feeling guilty. But men are not immune either. The reality is, without boundaries you are likely to lose your real self, your autonomy and your well-being in any relationship. Clients who come to see me to work on the unhealthy boundaries in their relationships are exhausted from the trap they find themselves in. They feel caught between knowing they need to change the imbalanced dynamic and feeling crippling guilt and fear at the prospect of activating their desired boundaries and stating their preferences. The codependence they feel has a tremendous grip on them. Their self-esteem rises and falls based on the other person's opinions, moods and tone of voice. Their emotions and limits are subjugated to other people's wants and needs. Their low self-value has the subconscious agenda of doing whatever the other person wants in order to not be abandoned and to be accepted.

As mentioned earlier, feeling and behaving like a hostage in a relationship is a common feeling when boundaries are unhealthy. People act in ways to avoid anger or conflict of any sort. Doing and saying things that are not authentic in order to be liked become the norm in a relationship without boundaries. People may find themselves loaning money they don't want to give and giving gifts or doing favors that are beyond their means, or that are inappropriate. Self-empowerment, therefore, takes a back seat, and resentment becomes the main currency in the relationship. With poor boundaries, relationships become a scary place, where people cannot relax and be genuine. Isolation becomes a preferred mode of self-protection. Conversely, clinging and doing whatever the other wants can also ensue. Either scenario is self-defeating.

Anatomy of a Good Boundary

The first and most important way to have a relationship that includes healthy boundaries is to be clear about how you feel about what you need and want. Do as much introspective work as possible, including journaling and therapy, in order to accomplish this. The habituation of having poor boundaries for a long time results in the numbing of one's true wants and needs. There is a loss of the important clues that feelings provide that will eventually generate a boundary. Instead of need and wants, other strong feelings show up; for example, constantly feeling angry, frustrated, hurt, resentful, boxed in, pushed, rebellious or victimized in a relationship is a sign that there are boundary issues in that relationship. Pay attention to what you are feeling. Don't just rationalize it away!

Marla came to see me about her relationships, and when we did closed-eyes work so that she was able to become introspective, she became aware of and revealed a deep-down resentment. Otherwise, she would say that she was not that aware of her feelings. She managed to function in life by numbing out. Eventually, she came to me for therapy because her buried feelings made her want to escape from her relationships without her knowing why. When we did the deeper work, we discovered the layers of boundary imbalances in her various work and personal relationships. With new awareness, she was able to slowly draw clearer boundaries that led her to feeling less angry and resentful.

Keep in mind when drawing boundaries in your relationships that it is very difficult to simultaneously create boundaries and take care of other people's feelings. People may feel hurt, taken aback or even angry when you set up boundaries, regardless of how you do the boundary-setting. All you can do is take care of yourself and try to communicate clearly but kindly and gently. A good tip is to set the boundary outside of an emotional setting; for example, if you are trying to get your partner to speak to you in public in a nonshaming way, I suggest that you create this boundary when the two of you are alone. Similarly, discuss boundaries about sex away from the bedroom. Before talking to the other person, practice saying what you want to say alone. It does get easier. Remember, we teach people how to treat us. The freedom one derives from boundary-setting is profound!

It is important to remember that setting boundaries is not about controlling your loved ones. The people you are setting boundaries with may say you are doing this, but they are just not used to your more empowered and vocal side. Drawing boundaries is more about defining what is acceptable to you and letting others know about it in a peaceful, clear and decided way. Consistency is a crucial aspect of sending a clear message that a new dynamic is taking place; also, very little will change if you set a boundary and then don't follow through. And remember, you are responsible only for your own feelings. It is important to disinvest from the outcome of a boundary-setting moment. You cannot please everyone all of the time.

Unhealthy and Healthy Boundaries

Following are examples of unhealthy and healthy boundaries to help you determine where you might need to make changes to improve your relationships.

Unhealthy Boundaries

1. I reveal everything about myself when I first meet someone.
2. I trust no one, or, I trust everyone.

3. I think in black and white and amputate people who disappoint me from my life.
4. I am overly generous to others so they will like me. I give beyond my ability.
5. I don't notice when someone invades my physical and emotional boundaries.
6. I allow others to direct my life, abandoning my values to please others.
7. I get mad when others do not fulfill my needs.
8. I am volatile when I get angry.
9. I have trouble and often get confused when making decisions.
10. I expect others to rescue me.

Healthy Boundaries

1. When I meet someone new, I make sure we are compatible before I reveal intimate aspects of myself. I take my time in deciding to let someone enter my world.
2. I trust people appropriately and take my time with that process.
3. I live in the gray, moving bit by bit into an intimate relationship. I understand people have flaws as well as virtues.
4. I give only when I choose to give. I respect myself. I don't use generosity as a tactic to manipulate others to like me.
5. I notice and speak out when others invade my physical and emotional boundaries.
6. I am the master of my life. I maintain a sense of my own values no matter what others are doing. I know my own truth and inner voice.

7. I know I have the right to ask others to fulfill my needs. But I also know they have a right to say no. I am gracious when others say no to me.
8. I have a right to my anger, but I know I always express my anger in responsible ways.
9. I know what is right for me. I am clear and grounded. I trust my decisions.
10. I avoid having expectations of others. I take care of myself. I treat myself as a kind and loving parent would treat me. I rescue myself.

Good Boundary Communication

Sometimes the words are just not there if you haven't practiced or been taught how to set good boundaries. Here are some examples of sentences you might use to create a good boundary when negotiating in a relationship:

- That sounds like a good idea, but I'm just not ready to do this at the moment.
- I'll give it some thought.
- I need time to consider what you are asking me to do. I'll get back to you tomorrow on that.
- I would appreciate your not yelling at me when you are angry. I'll listen to you if you speak calmly to me.
- I ask that you please lower your voice.
- That just doesn't work for me. Please stop it.
- When you speak to me like that, I feel belittled, judged and criticized. If this continues, I won't participate in this conversation. (And follow through!)
- ... is all I can take on. This is my limit.

- Please communicate with me calmly and honestly when we disagree. I won't participate in violent communication.
- I need to leave now. I'll speak to you later.
- I'm not ready yet. I need more time.
- This is who I am.

Baby steps at first are the name of the game. With time, good boundaries will be a real part of your life. A new normal is just around the corner. Be consistent. Be good to yourself. You need to fill your own cup first and give to others only from the overflow.

Defensiveness: The Relationship Killer!

So often I see people who chronically react defensively. This can put a damper on relationships, professional as well as personal. Defensive responses seem to come from a sense of superiority; however, they are, in fact, a cover-up for an inferiority complex or a feeling of insecurity.

Defensiveness can ruin relationships and destroy any sense of peacefulness and joy. People see defensive people as being touchy and having more boundaries than they need. The characteristics of defensive behavior include sarcasm, passive aggressiveness, immediately correcting the other person when they say something and responding in an opinionated, pointed manner. The attitude of the defensive person is one of "I'm here to tell you!"

If you find yourself feeling that you need to respond to someone defensively, stop and consider what is really going on. Often you will find that you are afraid of something: fear of being shamed, abandonment, rejection or being a subject of gossip. You perceive the other person as being on the attack or invading your space.

These fears are usually unfounded, and the other person had only made a comment that triggered something in you that somehow made you feel inadequate and that you were going to be judged, rejected or abandoned for that inadequacy.

When you find this defensive behavior in yourself, you need to work on it because it does not serve you well. The first thing to do is to change and stop the autopilot reaction so that you do not respond immediately when your buttons have been pushed. Don't be impulsive! You need to calm yourself by breathing deeply and steadily. Begin to count to yourself: one, two, three, four, five ... before you respond. Acknowledge to yourself what you are feeling, whether it is shame, hurt, fear of rejection or a negative vibe that you perceive from the other person. This acknowledgment will reduce the power of your need to be defensive. Acknowledgment is a healing, self-loving act toward yourself. It will actually empower you because it will put you in your truth, and whenever you are in your truth, you have more power. Defensiveness is disempowering because when you try to shut someone down, the repercussions can include feelings of guilt and remorse for your behavior. This leads to more shame and self-loathing, which are certainly disempowering. So any false power you were trying to garner from being defensive will backfire.

Jealousy in a Love Relationship

Darlene asked me about how to deal with the jealousy she was feeling in her happy and loving relationship. Unwarranted jealousy in a good relationship can quickly destroy it. She needed to look within herself for the answers to this difficult and self-sabotaging pattern.

Darlene told me about her turmoil-filled childhood, where her self-esteem was always under attack and she felt unsafe and insecure. Now that she was in a happy, positive and loving relationship with her boyfriend, she often felt jealous whenever female friends of her boyfriend came around, even though she knew that her feeling was illogical. Jealousy is often illogical; it comes from a place of deep insecurity, and it needs to be faced head-on. Darlene needed to discover what her perceived deficiency was. I asked her to begin journaling, and to do it often so she would get to know what made her tick, and what made her feel she was deficient in some way, even though the feeling was unwarranted.

She needed to discover how she might be benefitting from feeling jealous. At first glance, it is tough to find the benefit to a negative behavior, but there is. Jealousy can make people feel, on a subconscious level, as if they are taking care of themselves, protecting themselves from some kind of perceived harm. However, since her boyfriend had shown evidence over the years of being a good person and a good boyfriend, she didn't need to protect herself from him. But she did need to explore why she felt she was in need of self-protection. I suggested that in her journaling she explore the concept of the need to self-protect. I encouraged her to ask herself questions such as "How can I protect myself?" "How can I take care of me?" "What do I need to do?" "What have I neglected in my self-care?" "Have I not gone to the gym enough?" "Have I not taken my vitamins?" "Have I not taken time for myself?" "Am I running ragged?" "Am I disregarding my needs and who I am?" "Am I not complimenting myself?" "Am I not saying affirmations to myself?" "Am I constantly criticizing myself?"

In this way, Darlene began to understand the underlying causes of her pattern of jealousy. She had not been paying attention to her needs, and her self-care routine had gone by the wayside. This made her feel disconnected and insecure, which, in turn, brought on feelings of jealousy when she perceived her boyfriend to be paying attention to a seemingly more interesting woman. She would compare herself mercilessly with the other woman, and fights would ensue with her boyfriend, who felt that Darlene was accusing him of something he was not doing. Jealousy was no longer in the unconscious autopilot realm; it was now safely ensconced in her conscious mind, where it could be worked with and transformed. Remember, what is in your unconscious controls you, and what is in your conscious realm, you control.

I suggested to Darlene that she ground herself using the "Grounding Exercise" (which you can find in appendix VIII), every time she was going to be seeing her boyfriend so she could slow down enough to feel a connection with herself. Usually, unconscious, unwarranted behaviors show up when we are not grounded within ourselves. When we are grounded, we can develop feelings of self-connection, self-trust, self-worth and self-esteem.

In addition to centering and grounding herself, Darlene needed to restart her daily routines that made her feel good about herself. I also felt that it would be a good idea for her to take a breather from daily time spent with her boyfriend until she had dealt with her insecurities. Darlene needed time to take care of herself first; otherwise, she would continue to want from her boyfriend what she wasn't giving to herself.

In time, Darlene's relationship with her boyfriend improved, and she became aware that whenever her pattern of jealousy showed up it was because she had not been taking care of herself well enough. She knew that it was a sign that she needed to go back to caring for herself, journaling and doing breathing and grounding exercises so she would once again feel valuable, worthy and lovable.

New-Relationship Pitfalls

Picture this: You have met a new person recently, and you are instantly "in love." You want to spend all day and night with this person. You feel as if you are drugged with this person's energy, and you cannot get enough. You need your daily fix and will do whatever it takes to keep the feeling alive. You love every little thing about the person, and you don't limit one bit the length of time you are together. Self-culture? What self-culture? Personal activities, hobbies, family and friends go by the wayside as the new romance takes over every part of your life. As time passes, you begin to see each other as you really are—each other's flaws. You have your first fight. Even though you both sincerely felt the deepness of the connection at the beginning, the honeymoon has worn off; now the real work begins. The adventure of entering into a new relationship can be sensational and wondrous. However, it can also be challenging to navigate in an emotionally safe way unless you are clear about and aware of self-culture and what is actually happening in the relationship.

Let's look at that initial seeming addiction to one another. That is the biochemical oxytocin in action. This "nesting hormone" courses through both parties' veins and increases every time they touch, caress and even more every time they make love. I usually caution my clients against having sex too soon in a relationship due to this pernicious little hormone that can trick the mind into thinking it wants to build a nest with someone, even if the person may not be right for them. This oxytocin hit can make people ignore clear signs of dysfunction. It can override clear logic, self-care, healthy boundaries and appropriate romance time management that leads people to abandon themselves, their friends and activities that are outside the relationship's inner sanctum!

A good rule of thumb is to slow the physical intimacy down enough for the emotional intimacy to catch up. We need trust, familiarity, consistency, respect and a proven track record to be authentic and relaxed. That requires time. Rushing into the physical and sensual realms too quickly can result in emotionally rough waters. Stick your toe in first. Test the water. And then move slowly into it as you become comfortable. That way the hormone love drug will not trick you into falling hopelessly in love with Mr. or Ms. Wrong!

An essential component to navigating safely in new relationships is having good and healthy boundaries. The trouble is, most people have a hard time knowing what good boundaries are. Impulsiveness, for example, can indicate poor boundaries. In the case of new relationships, slow is always better if you are to care well for yourself and your soul. Try not to reveal too much of yourself all at once. Move slowly, checking for compatibility and a sense of safety first.

Once the relationship progresses past the honeymoon phase, it is best not to get caught up in the disease-to-please. Good boundaries are saying yes only when you want to do something and no when you do not want to. Remember, we are not responsible for how the other person feels, only for how we feel. If you develop authentic yeses and no's, there is less of a chance of building resentment walls that are sure to create emotional scar tissue in the relationship. Also, personalize your self-care. Find out what you need and desire, then take personal responsibility for it. You are the expert on yourself. Try not to make the other person responsible for your happiness.

Check within yourself to see if you are falling for the person just because they are reaching out to you. If you do this, it may indicate that you are not looking at your own value and worth in a bid to avert loneliness. Commit to being true and authentic to yourself at all times. This may mean risking letting someone go. But waiting for the right person to fall in love with is so rewarding and definitely worth staying the course of commitment to self. Remember that like attracts like, and when you are in the vibration of self-love and self-respect, you are bound to attract a similar vibration in someone else. Have the intention to be true to yourself.

As the relationship evolves, pay attention to what the other person is doing versus what they are saying. "Show, don't tell" is the philosophy. Believe people when they show you who they are. Don't slip into a blissful oxytocin-induced denial of what is really going on. You really can't trust words in a new relationship. It's all about actions. Do not ignore the signs and symptoms of key warning flags. Don't fall in love with someone's potential! Pay attention to what you see in the here and now. Staying in a relationship based on what you think the other person may become is a tremendously tempting hazard that usually seriously disappoints!

Stay true to your own core values despite what someone else may want; otherwise, feelings of self-betrayal may ensue. Compromise is needed in many areas as the relationship becomes more serious, but it is crucial to be the person you truly are versus whom you would like to present, especially at the beginning. Also, don't bring old patterns of behavior into the new relationship. Emotional projections and baggage from past hurts or past failed relationships can sabotage the future of a new and emerging connection.

The reality is that we grow the most through relationships. New ones are a worthwhile risk that needs to be taken with your eyes wide open. Lessons will be learned no matter what, but the above guidelines may facilitate the navigation of the new relationship journey with a little more ease.

Chapter Thirteen

COMMITMENT PHOBIA

Commitment phobia is a very painful experience for the person who engages in the pattern, as well as for those who are involved with that person. Usually, the art of seduction, and then the exercise of "push-pull," are the domain of the "commitment-phobe." The cause dwells deeply in the survival patterns of a person's family of origin.

In my practice, I often see people—women and men—with commitment phobia. The key characteristic is fear—fear of intimacy and deep emotional connection. People who are commitment phobic feel they need to cut off their feelings after a certain point in a relationship so they can feel they are in control and are emotionally protected. Often they are not even conscious of what they are doing as it occurs deep in their subconscious.

Commitment-phobes are hard to spot because they are skilled in the art of seduction; however, if you know what you are looking for, you can spot a commitment-phobe a mile away. At first, they are caught up in the thrill of the hunt. They love to pursue and seduce, but once they "get" the person, they lose interest. They begin to keep score, meticulously picking out the negative traits in the other person. I am not saying people should ignore negative traits, or stay in relationships they're not happy in, but with the commitment-phobic person, this seeking out of negative traits in the other person is particularly acute and almost obsessive.

Commitment-phobes look for perfection, which they erroneously feel will make them happy, in control and, ultimately, emotionally safe. When they find someone whom they feel would measure up, the push-pull journey begins. They are there, and then they are not. The person is fully present, full of compliments and sweet nothings, and then they don't call for days. You know—the disappearing act! And when they are there, they are always thinking about how they might escape out the backdoor.

A very unhappy commitment-phobic client once said, "I'm not here for a long time, but I'm here for a good time, so I'm going to be very seductive and very romantic with her. But as soon as I get a whiff that she is starting to relax with me, be more human and real with me, I'm outta here!" Through therapy, we learned that he did this repeatedly, and, as a result, he suffered from loneliness, which is why he sought out a therapist; however, he couldn't change the pattern, even with awareness. His parents had divorced, and there had been great instability throughout his childhood, which led him to constantly work to mitigate future pain. He was unable to just be in the moment and enjoy a new love relationship. He needed to always feel one step ahead. He was deeply concerned about being "trapped" by a woman who might depend on him in any way, and he perceived any form of intimacy as a trap.

Another difficult case was a woman who had dated, and even become engaged to, a covert commitment-phobe. He had promised her a rose garden for years, and one month before the wedding, when all the plans had been made and all the guests had confirmed their attendance, he checked out emotionally. She became aware of what was happening and called off the wedding. If she had not finally woken up and begun to piece together his symptoms and realized he was a commitment-phobe, they might have made it to the wedding day, only to have him leave her standing alone at the altar.

During the relationship, there had been signs and symptoms of the commitment phobia, but she had been in denial about it. He had refused to move in with her, even though they were in their late thirties, employed and had been together many years. He deferred to the opinions of his very controlling mother, whom he lived with. Sometimes he went for days without answering her calls. And then, when she finally gave up, he would show up with a lavish bouquet of flowers and try to seduce and cajole her into softening her anger over his absence, which he would never explain. He would just tell her to live in the present and "not spoil the beautiful moment I have planned for us." She knew deep down that something was off, and so, as the wedding day approached, she gathered her courage and decided to question him about what he was truly feeling. She did not relent, and he finally admitted that he was not going to go through with the wedding. This devastated her, but it was also a relief for her to finally hear the truth. She felt a wave of relaxation come over her knowing that she was not crazy after all. She felt he had seduced her and then strung her along. He maintained that he did this so he wouldn't "hurt" her. He had felt that lying was a better option, even though he planned on making a last-minute wedding-day bail out! Classic commitment phobia!

Look out for people who are constantly looking at other people while on a date with you. Also be mindful that commitment-phobic people are born salespeople; they can spin a web and tell a story that is unparalleled. What is actually happening is that they are usually covering their lies with the stories. Commitment-phobes do not really want to hurt people. They are trying to prevent themselves from getting hurt, and they have the delusion that they can have it all. They feel accomplished when they realize they can lie and get away with it. They feel as though they are winning when they are able to spin a story that is believable. They are in control. They have the upper hand. I have learned that they actually believe their own tales, and they have clearly rationalized the need to tell these tales. They are addicted to the excitement of lying. Sometimes some form of sexual addiction is mixed in with commitment phobia. However, it is not always this dramatic; sometimes the person is just unable to settle into a good relationship, and they break it off as soon as it becomes monogamous and, to them, monotonous. Either way, being involved with a commitment-phobic person is not healthy or a good idea for anyone.

When I work with commitment-phobic people, I realize that they themselves are not at all in touch with their inner truths. I ask the question, "So why do you think you're doing this?" And the answer invariably is, "I don't know. I'm not sure." They are cut off from their own emotions because they are afraid of them. Reality and the authentic, gritty truths are tough for many people to accept, but for the person who is commitment phobic, it is nearly impossible for them to face the emotions associated with delving into deep truths. They have developed a protective layer that keeps them riding the surface of their personality, and they never analyze their true inner motivations. The good news is that if a person is a commitment-phobe, and they make contact with their own suffering as well as the suffering that they foist on others, they have a chance to shift, but it is a long and arduous path out of this deeply ingrained pattern of behavior.

I caution you to not get involved with someone you suspect is commitment phobic because, if a long-term commitment is what you are after, this kind of person is sure to hurt you! It won't be a pretty situation unless you yourself are a commitment-phobic person as well. We know that like attracts like, so that may also be a likely scenario; in fact, it might be a good temporary match, since both parties are not interested in a long-term commitment. However, denial is not just a river in Egypt! I know of a commitment-phobic couple who got married in Las Vegas within one week of knowing each other because they got caught up in the romance of it all. The intensity of the connection had made them slip into denial, which seduced them into deciding to marry. Of course, the marriage did not last, and much pain ensued! The same scenario is possible when a commitment-phobe is in a relationship with a clingy person. This is a match made in hell; they are seduced by romance and destroyed by codependency and low self-worth on both sides.

Commitment-phobic people tend to grow up in volatile, emotionally unsafe families, or in families where the parents are in a loveless, silent relationship. In either case, the tension, unhappiness and dissatisfaction are palpable, and everyone just wants out. In the case of the loud and volatile family, the children become insecure, not knowing what will happen the next day, or what mood the mother or father will be in at any given time. Sometimes this is due to one or both parents having an addiction of some sort, such as alcoholism. The kids are never relaxed and develop a state of being in which they feel they always have to have one foot in and one foot out. Can you imagine a child being completely invested in a mother or father whom they cannot trust? The child is in a constant state of panic. This volatile, unstable home creates a neural-pathway belief system to be commitment phobic. "Why am I going to commit when it has been unsafe to commit only to people whom I'm supposed to trust and relax with?" On the other hand, children who grew up in a silent, loveless and unexpressive home had no role model for healthy, committed adult attachments either. They have no idea what healthy emotional bonding feels like. For those of you who are commitment phobic and want to get over it, you need to engage in therapy to discover the influences of your family of origin because, clearly, if you had a choice, you probably wouldn't be doing this. Your awareness and consciousness level aren't sufficient for you to move beyond this on your own. I invite you to engage in a process of self-analysis and therapy. Journaling and meditation are a good start. Get in touch with what makes you act in ways that clearly hurt other people and yourself.

In my opinion, being in a relationship provides us with an opportunity to learn and to grow the most. I am not saying that when you are single you can't learn a lot, but when you are in a relationship, there is an opportunity to learn the discipline required to get through general boredom, sexual boredom and immature impulsiveness. It allows a person the space to be vulnerable, open and insecure in front of their partner, which can then cultivate a sense of deep trust. These qualities are tremendously stimulating for the growth of the soul. Our souls look to find opportunities to become more vulnerable, more open, more trusting, less suspicious and less escapist. We are relationship-oriented as humans, and I think that in relationships we tend to grow the most and learn our spiritual lessons more profoundly.

Quick Tips for the Commitment-Phobic Person

- Be in the present moment; be right here, right now with the person in front of you. See what is good and right in the relationship now! (This is especially important for those of you in your child-bearing years who want to start to build a life with somebody.)
- Know and accept that nothing and no one are perfect!
- If your family was dysfunctional, become aware of how your parents behaved and find ways to do the opposite.
- Read the book *He's Scared, She's Scared: Understanding the Hidden Fears That Sabotage Your Relationships* by Steven Carter and Julia Sokol.
- Practice meditation regularly as a way to calm anxiety. Escaping intimacy is often used as a means to calm anxiety; if this is the case, meditation can help to calm the feelings that lead you to sabotage your relationships.
- Work to be honest with the person you are in a relationship with.
- Decide that not leading anyone on is a rule you live by.
- Engage in therapy so you have someone to confide in and can learn more about yourself and your patterns.

Chapter Fourteen

THE CODEPENDENT LIFE

We live in a culture in which codependency seems to be normal. The very relationships that are labeled as good, healthy and normal in the media are, in many cases, unhealthy, overenmeshed, compromised and lacking in freedom and joy. When we scratch below the surface, we see patterns of unhappiness stemming from entrenched manipulation, including lying to self and deceiving the partner, toxic guilt and shame and, worst of all, resentment and deep unhappiness later in the relationship. This applies not only to love relationships but also to parent-child, sibling, co-worker, friendship and boss-employee relationships. All relationships have the potential to be codependent. It is important to look at the road that may have led a relationship from profound ebullient love or getting along great to deep resentment and eventual breakup. The breakup may not be physical, but it will be emotional. This is a deeper parting that creates trauma and profound pain for the participants because they usually stay connected far too long but are profoundly unhappy when the disease of codependency is in full swing.

The most common thread in a codependent relationship is that one or both in the partnership consistently does not make themselves a priority. Self is second to the other. This sounds like a desirable state of being given the Judeo-Christian roots of our culture. But the reality is that this type of extreme undermining of self in favor of the other never lands in a good place. The self-esteem of one or both is deeply compromised; it rises and falls based on the other person's mood, tone, need, disposition or actions. In the face of such volatile emotions, codependents find themselves trying to predict or circumvent the changing landscape. Ultimately, this is crazy-making for all. No one has a real grasp on what their true feelings are. The disease-to-please pattern is deeply held and all-encompassing.

Where Does Codependence Begin?

Those who are preoccupied with the other's needs came by this hyperawareness honestly. They learned very early in life that they needed to tune into others and their needs or there would be consequences. This messaging came about through growing up in an environment in which they needed to perform to get love or attention. Perhaps they observed anger or mocking, or they were simply ignored. At three months to two years of age, our sense of our environment is acute. This is when our needs are the main priority in the relationship, so if children sense that those needs are not being met in the way they need them to be, they unconsciously begin questioning if they deserve to be tended to. They become apathetic about and disconnected from their own needs. They develop a why-bother-asking attitude. On the one hand, they want to take up as little space and air time as possible so as not to "bother" their parents. On the other hand, they may become highly self-sufficient too early; for example, they may begin to walk and talk very early in a bid to become as self-reliant as possible as quickly as possible since their caregivers wouldn't tend to their needs. These children are always trying to please to keep the parent from being angry, sad or mean. This self-sufficiency hails from a deep hurt brewing within that harkens to the questions

"Am I worth being paid attention to?" and "Am I worth being alive and loved?" These questions are lodged deep in the unconscious, waiting to be expressed at a later time in other relationships.

The Addiction

Later in life, codependency patterns appear and an undercurrent of profound nervousness comes about if people dare to do what they want to do in the face of opposing wants. It is their conditioning in action. They may not even be aware that this is their pattern; they just know they are not at all comfortable asking for what they need. They find it painful to listen to their own needs. As their personality evolves, the not knowing what they truly need and want is always there. The other person's wants are what the real demand of the moment is. Anything short of that is a problem for them. I have seen full-on anxiety attacks when a person attempts to tune into their own needs and wants. In this sense, codependency is a form of addiction that is ruled by compulsive actions to avoid the pain of self-care. That is, a preoccupation with the other's feelings, problems and situations is activated as a way to mitigate the pain of feeling their own needs and the fear that they will be rejected or disappointed. There is also a "high," and their self-esteem also gets a boost when they make another person happy.

Aren't We All Codependent?

A common question might be, "Isn't everyone codependent?" We all have codependent tendencies within us if we feel empathy and compassion toward other people. But the question is, do we engage in relationships in which our empathy for another becomes so much higher than our own self-care that the other person consumes our minds and takes up space in a way that our own needs are sidelined? To determine whether or not you are in a codependent relationship, you need to analyze your motivation for your feelings of empathy. Are they driven by fear of rejection, abandonment or criticism; the need to fix someone; feelings of guilt; feeling you need to protect yourself; or the need to have control over the environment? These are not free and healthy motivations; they are compulsive responses, akin to a fix from a drug. This is the "sick" side of love.

What Does the Codependent Relationship Look Like?

You need to keep in mind that in the beginning, everyone feels wonderful in codependent relationships because both parties hang on every word the other says and tend to the other's every need and emotion. At first, the relationship seems cozy and the couple is in tune with one another. But the lovely song soon becomes nightmarishly discordant. The dark side emerges as guilt and control rule the environment. This is where deception comes in. Codependent people are so consumed with not hurting the other person that they become obsessed with showing only a side of themselves that is palatable and positive. They constantly playact a version of themselves. They bury their authentic selves, but their true selves are only asleep, waiting to be expressed. Codependent people feel that they have to conceal their real selves, which leaves them having to play out their inner desires in rogue and hidden ways, such as having affairs, acting wild and telling lies. In codependent relationships, boundaries are crossed with deplorable treatment, passive-aggressiveness, sarcasm and controlling behavior, all of which might be explained away as moods or phases. In the codependent relationship, one person takes over the other's life, and the other allows them to do it. All of this then builds to a crescendo over years of self-denial as toxic guilt and shame pervade after years of living a lie. It is common for codependent people to always be apologizing for even existing at all!

Some Key Codependent Traits

Co-Dependents Anonymous lists some patterns and characteristics of codependency that may assist you in determining if you are, in fact, a codependent type of person or if you are in a codependent relationship. Ask yourself if any of the following apply to you:[1]

Denial Patterns

- I have difficulty identifying what I am feeling.
- I minimize, alter, or deny how I truly feel.
- I perceive myself as completely unselfish and dedicated to the well-being of others.
- I lack empathy for the feelings and needs of others.
- I label others with my negative traits.
- I can take care of myself without any help from others.
- I mask my pain in various ways such as anger, humor, or isolation.
- I express negativity or aggression in indirect and passive ways.
- I do not recognize the unavailability of those people to whom I am attracted.

Low Self-Esteem Patterns

- I have difficulty making decisions.
- I judge what I think, say, or do harshly, as never good enough.

---

1 Reprinted from *Patterns and Characteristics of Codependence* with the permission of Co-Dependents Anonymous, Inc.

- I am embarrassed to receive recognition, praise, or gifts.
- I value others' approval of my thinking, feelings, and behavior over my own.
- I do not perceive myself as a lovable or worthwhile person.
- I constantly seek recognition that I think I deserve.
- I have difficulty admitting that I made a mistake.
- I need to appear to be right in the eyes of others and will even lie to look good.
- I am unable to ask others to meet my needs or desires.
- I perceive myself as superior to others.
- I look to others to provide my sense of safety.
- I have difficulty getting started, meeting deadlines, and completing projects.
- I have trouble setting healthy priorities.

Compliance Patterns

- I am extremely loyal, remaining in harmful situations too long.
- I compromise my own values and integrity to avoid rejection or anger.
- I put aside my own interests in order to do what others want.
- I am hypervigilant regarding the feelings of others and take on those feelings.
- I am afraid to express my beliefs, opinions, and feelings when they differ from those of others.
- I accept sexual attention when I want love.
- I make decisions without regard to the consequences.
- I give up my truth to gain the approval of others or to avoid change.

Control Patterns

- I believe most people are incapable of taking care of themselves.
- I attempt to convince others what to think, do, or feel.

- I freely offer advice and direction to others without being asked.
- I become resentful when others decline my help or reject my advice.
- I lavish gifts and favors on those I want to influence.
- I use sexual attention to gain approval and acceptance.
- I have to be needed in order to have a relationship with others.
- I demand that my needs be met by others.
- I use charm and charisma to convince others of my capacity to be caring and compassionate.
- I use blame and shame to emotionally exploit others.
- I refuse to cooperate, compromise, or negotiate.
- I adopt an attitude of indifference, helplessness, authority, or rage to manipulate outcomes.
- I use terms of recovery in an attempt to control the behavior of others.
- I pretend to agree with others to get what I want.

Avoidance Patterns

- I act in ways that invite others to reject, shame, or express anger toward me.
- I judge harshly what others think, say, or do.
- I avoid emotional, physical, or sexual intimacy as a means of maintaining distance.
- I allow my addictions to people, places, and things to distract me from achieving intimacy in relationships.
- I use indirect and evasive communication to avoid conflict or confrontation.
- I diminish my capacity to have healthy relationships by declining to use all the tools of recovery.
- I suppress my feelings or needs to avoid feeling vulnerable.

- I pull people toward me, but when they get close, I push them away.
- I refuse to give up my self-will to avoid surrendering to a power that is greater than myself.
- I believe displays of emotion are a sign of weakness.
- I withhold expressions of appreciation.

If these patterns and characteristics apply to you, it would be a good idea to visit a codependency support group as well as read any books by Melody Beattie, including *Codependent No More: How to Stop Controlling Others and Start Caring for Yourself*. Codependency has far-reaching and destructive consequences that need to be neutralized as soon as possible, and therapy can be very helpful for this condition.

Work diligently to strengthen your self-esteem through profound and courageous self-care. Always question your motives for the decisions you make regarding your relationships. Ask yourself why you are doing what you are doing. Is it to gain approval? Is it to please someone? Is it to be liked? Is it to avoid loneliness? Is it to get what you missed from your family of origin? Know that no matter what, others cannot fill the void inside you. You have to do that job yourself. You have to change the dynamic between yourself and the person you are with through new actions and new behavior patterns. Choose to be an actor and not a reactor. Choose not to engage in drama and enmeshing dynamics. Choose self-care over self-sabotage. Choose self-acceptance over self-annihilation.

Can There Be Commitment without Codependency?

The key to a healthy and committed relationship is a feeling of deep and real love plus freedom. Each person in the relationship needs to feel free to express themselves without fear of judgment, abandonment or rejection. There needs to be a freedom for each person to be and do what they want without fear of reprisals. Ideally, each person in the relationship is strong and has enough self-esteem so they do not need to control, manipulate or lie to the other, or subjugate themselves either. It is a connection based on mutual respect, chemistry and, of course, the almighty freedom to be their authentic selves. This ideal can be achieved through profound awareness and unearthing the deep inner needs and wants of the true self that may have been buried for a very long time. Recovery from codependency is possible with consistent and persistent work on the issue and on the addictive side of this condition. Therapy and group support are tools that help. You need to realize that you matter and that your needs are important. Self-care is the answer and the way out of the codependent life.

Chapter Fifteen

ANXIETY: COPING WITH A GOLIATH OF OUR TIME

"Didn't you know that anxiety is the new normal?" That is what a client flippantly said to me one day. She was trying to be funny, but we both knew it came from pure frustration and feeling overwhelmed. So many people today seem to be tormented by anxiety in one form or another, including social anxiety. Clients have told me that they have a primal fear of anxiety because it has the power to paralyze them in a one-two punch, no matter what their good intentions might be. Without management, anxiety causes people to lose their sense of joy, purpose and stability in life.

Possible root causes can be a lack of stability in childhood, which may overactivate a person's worry center in the brain. Genetics can also play a role in the puzzle of anxiety. Ultimately, there are many possible sources for anxiety that can at times be perplexing. An unstable childhood that is rife with violent communication, volatility, addiction and trauma (physical as well as emotional) can cause stress to the nervous system that results in the child and, subsequently, the adult being in a constant state of hypervigilance and overreactivity. In a turbulent family, the child has to cope with a landscape that is constantly changing. And since we tend to form our worldview by the time we are six or seven years old, this state of never knowing what is around the corner, or always waiting for the other shoe to drop, can develop into severe anxiety in adulthood.

Family dynamics, such as lack of acknowledgment; always being judged; being criticized; lack of respect for boundaries; emotional blackmail; passive-aggressiveness; and cold, nonverbal interaction among family members may all be potential breeding grounds for the development of anxiety patterns later in life. The "hard-working baby" results when a child perceives that he or she needs to work hard for attention, acceptance, love and recognition. An urgent need for closeness and belonging evolves, or a fear of abandonment unfolds, which may turn into a constant need to perform, apologize, be perfect, be good and be likeable in order to get what they seek. The anxiety of not getting what they need is the constant undercurrent.

In addition, when children grow up feeling that they are not safe, their survival instincts cause them to produce "biochemicals of trauma," which can result in chemical imbalances in the brain that cause cognitive distortions later in life.

That said, people who had a traumatic family life as children don't necessarily have chronic anxiety when they grow up. People deal with these types of early childhood experiences in different ways. Anxiety tends to run in families, and we tend to inherit this predisposition. So if all the pieces are there, the proverbial fertile soil to develop such a condition may ensue. But not necessarily.

Anxiety is physically uncomfortable. It is at times uncontrollable. There may be sweating, stuttering, worrying and obsessing, and some people experience heart palpitations, faster breathing, panicky feelings, lost feelings, clinginess, paranoia and more. Logic has a hard time surpassing these anxiety patterns. The brain has developed thick neural pathways that reflect this type of mental, emotional and physical response to deep-seated trauma.

The good news is that there are a variety of strategies for coping with anxiety. This is crucial not only to improve the sufferers' quality of life but also to prevent their immune systems from becoming compromised by the stress of this perceived Goliath.

Eleven Powerful Tools to Help You Cope with Anxiety

1. **Breathing.** Deep, slow and conscious breathing is by far the simplest, least-expensive and most-effective tool for quickly stimulating the relaxation response of the parasympathetic nervous system when you are feeling anxious. Breathing can begin the slow but sure journey of building the relaxation neural pathways that are crucial to interrupting the autopilot anxiety response. Getting used to catching yourself just when you are beginning to feel anxious, and then consciously and deliberately slowing down your breathing, will decelerate your heart rate and your mind. Breathing will gently shift your focus back to a safe space. There are many breathing techniques, but a simple one is to put your hand on your stomach and slowly breathe in to a count of three and out to a count of three. Slowly increase the count to four in and four out, and then to five in and five out, increasing the count as far as you feel comfortable.
2. **Tense and relax your muscles.** Start with your arms. Take one arm and stretch it out while tensing it for five or six seconds. Then relax the arm. Do this with each limb, then your jaw, your stomach, and work your way around all parts of your body. It has a remarkable easing influence on the entire body.

3. **Visualization.** Positive, relaxing visualization capitalizes on the fact that your brain does not seem to differentiate between real or perceived events. Creating a peaceful place in nature in your mind, such as a beach, mountain, waterfall, garden or forest, and focusing on it in great detail can be very effective for calming anxiety when it is done habitually. It will stimulate the relaxation response in the same way as deep, slow breathing does. In therapy sessions with my clients, I often facilitate their creation of this safe, peaceful space, where they can visualize their setting in nature in great detail so they can easily recreate the visual whenever they are feeling anxious. Visualization is like a muscle that needs to be practiced regularly to remain useful and facilitate the creation of these particularly important neural pathways that calm the worry center down.
4. **Create an anxiety thought log.**[1] When you feel anxious, record your thoughts on a sheet of paper or in a journal. At the first sign of anxiety, breathe slowly and, as soon as possible, find a quiet place to sit down and process the event and your thoughts on paper. Begin by describing the following:
   i. What was the situation? Who was I with? Where was I? When did it happen?
   ii. What was my mood like? What were all my feelings while it was happening? List all the feelings you experienced and still feel regarding the situation that caused the anxiety; for example, sad, scared, judged, resentful, angry or any other feeling that comes up. Once you have done this, rate the intensity of each feeling from one to ten, with one being the least intense and ten being the most intense.

---

1 This exercise is adapted from the book *Mind over Mood: Change How You Feel by Changing How You Think* by Dennis Greenberger and Christine A. Padesky.

iii. Discover what your automatic thoughts were by asking yourself the following: What was going through my mind just before I started to feel anxious? What was I afraid would happen? What was the worst thing that I was worried about in the situation? What words, pictures and memories come to me as I think of the situation?
iv. Then ask yourself: What evidence do I have to support these worrying and fearful thoughts? (Avoid interpreting other people's thoughts. You are not a mind reader.)
v. Then ask: What evidence do I have that does not support these worrying and fearful thoughts? Challenge the fearful thoughts. Use logic and reality-based thinking as much as possible.
vi. To discover more balanced thoughts about the situation, circle each negative, fearful thought you discover and create a separate page that states the opposite, more balanced and empowered thought. For example, if you wrote, "I am afraid people will hate me if I say what I think," on a separate page write, "Other people's opinions are theirs. It is safe and good to speak my truth. I am lovable and strong even when I don't think I am."
vii. Once you have completed this exercise, go back and look at the original feelings you wrote down and rate the intensity of the feelings again. Hopefully, they will have come down in intensity as you go through this process. (You may need to do it a couple of times to decrease the intensity further.) Tune into any new feelings that come up and write them down. Feelings such as calmness, clarity and groundedness may show up after the process.

5. **Separate what you have control over from what you do not.** Know that you do not have control over outcomes and other people's reactions and actions. You do have control over your own thoughts, feelings and perspectives on life. Work on those.
6. **Don't overwhelm yourself.** Deal with one thing at a time. Keep life simple. Know your limitations and don't take on more than you can handle.
7. **Take supplements that support brain health.** Essential fatty acids (EFAs) are natural mood boosters and have a calming effect;[2] take at least 4,000 mg of the EFAs EPA and DHA combined. A good way to take it is 2,000 mg in the morning and 2,000 mg at night. A good vitamin B complex (100 mg of each B vitamin) has been shown to be beneficial to adults with depression.[3] Vitamin D, at least 2,000 IUs per day, works to elevate mood and disposition.[4] In addition, the amino acid 5-hydroxytryptophan (5-HTP) is the precursor to the feel-good hormone serotonin;[5] take 100 to 200 mg in the morning and 100 to 200 mg at night to help with sleep.

---

2 Maria Baroy Raeder et al., "Associations between Cod Liver Oil Use and Symptoms of Depression: The Hordaland Health Study," *Journal of Affective Disorders* 101, nos. 1–3 (2007): 245–249.

3. John E. Lewis et al., "The Effect of Methylated Vitamin B Complex on Depressive and Anxiety Symptoms and Quality of Life in Adults with Depression," *ISRN Psychiatry* Available at: www.hindawi.com/isrn/psychiatry/2013/621453.

4 F. Michael Gloth 3rd, Wasif Alam, and Bruce Hollis, "Vitamin D vs Broad Spectrum Phototherapy in the Treatment of Seasonal Affective Disorder," *Journal of Nutrition Health and Aging* 3, no. 1 (1999): 5–7.

5 Timothy C. Birdsall, "5-Hydroxytryptophan: A Clinically Effective Serotonin Precursor," *Alternative Medicine Review* 3, no. 4 (1998): 271–280.

Please note that 5-HTP must not be taken if you are already taking an allopathic antidepressant. Also make sure you do not take it on an empty stomach to prevent stomach upset. Inositol, also known as vitamin B8, is an excellent antianxiety nutrient;[6,7] take 8 to 10 g per day in powdered form; Advanced Orthomolecular Research (A.O.R.) is an excellent brand. Lorna Vanderhaeghe has a line of products that I like called ADRENAsmart. She combines herbs, including the all-important rhodiola, that go to work to calm the nervous system. Follow the instructions on the bottle. It is very effective for anxiety. Rescue Remedy is a wonderful combination of flower remedies that helps calm a person down when they are anxious.[8] I recommend you keep it in your purse or pocket at all times.

8. **Exercise.** Exercise stimulates the release of endorphins and, therefore, plays an important role in feeling good about yourself and life. It helps to maintain calmness within and is a good stress reliever.
9. **Become aware of the present moment.** Notice your internal running commentary. Are you constantly focusing on worst-case scenarios? Begin to encourage yourself to create a constant positive running commentary about life in general. Notice your inner thinking while doing mundane activities. Affirm that "everything is working out better than I expected."

6 Alex Palatnik et al., "Double-Blind, Controlled, Crossover Trial of Inositol versus Fluvoxamine for the Treatment of Panic Disorder," *Journal of Clinical Psychopharmacology* 21, no. 3 (2001): 335–339.

7 Joseph Levine, "Controlled Trials of Inositol in Psychiatry," *European Neuropsychoparmacology* 7, no. 2 (1997): 147–155.

8 Robert Halberstein et al., "Healing with Bach® Flower Essences: Testing a Complementary Therapy," *Complementary Health Practice Review* 12, no. 3 (2007): 3–13.

10. **Don't rush.** Leave time for yourself when going somewhere. Being in a rushed state will often trigger anxiety.
11. **Get in touch with the child within you.** Parent your inner child as you wish you had been treated as a child. Give your inner child what he or she needs: love, acceptance, relaxation, respect, empowerment, nurturing, good choices and safety, all unconditionally.

Detail-Observation Exercise

One of the most important ways to calm your mind during an anxiety episode is to stop and focus on the details. Wherever you are, find an object around you that you can concentrate on. Trace everything about it—its lines, curves, shape, texture, colors—every detail. I have a wall of diplomas in my office, and when a client is having an anxiety episode, I have them trace with their eyes all the lines, curls and other nuances they see on the wall. The more detail the better.

When you focus on detail like this, you will notice that your breathing starts to slow down, and the longer you do it, the better. If you are somewhere that has few details to concentrate on, then just look at your hand; it has a plethora of lines and other details for you to focus on. As you observe the details of your hand, notice your mind calming down and your breathing slowing.

This exercise also works for phobias. I have a client who is very afraid of getting her blood drawn because she is afraid of needles. I worked with her on this exercise, and now she is able to take a needle without fainting. The detail exercise helps her to focus her thoughts, which, in turn, calms her whole being.

When you focus on details, your mind shifts away from scary, anxious thoughts. It also brings you squarely into the present moment and out of future-worrying or past-dwelling.

Anxiety is often about not having a good emotional, physical or logical grasp on your environment. Your emotions are distorted when you engage in future-worrying, and focusing on the details of your environment orients you. It creates an opportunity for your mind to settle and begin to touch upon logical thinking. Your brain begins to step out of the reptilian fight-or-flight response and goes into the more logical aspect of the adult brain.

Submarine Exercise

When you feel anxious, your body may respond by tightening, even though you have no idea as to what caused your anxiety. At these times, stop, sit down and close your eyes. Imagine a tiny submarine entering your body and you are in the submarine. Use your imagination to direct the submarine to the tight and tense place in your body and hover there. You are the captain, and you are driving the submarine. You have the ability to communicate with your body just by sending it your thoughts. Notice that as you do this, you begin to calm down. Give yourself the space to ask the tense part of your body, "What is this tension all about?" Pause and wait for the answers to emerge. Very soon you will have information that is buried there. A fear, fleeting worry or passing paranoia about something that may have been vague or you were too busy to cognitively process often shows up.

This exercise gives you a chance to hear what your anxiety is all about, instead of its being just a heap of feelings that are all mixed up and overwhelming. As soon as the answer comes, you will feel a sense of relief and a loosening of the tension. You can then dialogue with this tightness. For example, you can feed yourself positive and logical information such as "I hear you are worried about what that person is thinking about you, but, in truth, what other people think is not my business," or "I hear you are obsessing about what happened before, but the past is over. We are in the present moment now, and all is well and safe."

When you slow down your cognitive brain, you are more able to be reasonable and rational about what triggered your anxiety. This is an opportunity for your mind to become disciplined by your intention. If your intention is to calm yourself down, then this is a great way to effortlessly begin going in that direction.

White-Light Exercise

A good way to create calmness within yourself, especially when you are in a new environment or you are stepping into a situation that is familiar but anxiety-provoking, is to imagine that a dome of white protective light is surrounding you. Take a moment to visualize the creation of a wonderfully safe dome that you place around yourself. Once in the dome, allow your mind to focus on a feeling of ease as you make contact with other people. This may give you a sense that you can be in contact with others without feeling invaded by what you perceive they may be thinking or doing. Anxiety can make a person overly sensitive to others, and this visualization assists in mitigating the need to be overly reactive to other people. Practice taking the dome with you as you navigate the different events of your life.

I also suggest visualizing yourself putting a white light over other people. Take the time to visualize a person you care about being protected by this dome of white light. For example, an anxious parent can visualize himself or herself putting a white light over their child as the child walks to school, or as the child enters the car-pool vehicle, or a friend may visualize himself or herself putting a white light over a friend who is undergoing an operation. This act of sending the energy of protection to watch over those you care about may calm the anxiety that is triggered by your worry over others.

Leaning Out!

You need mental discipline to cope with anxiety. When anxiety shows up, we tend to be overly controlling and place obsessive attention on perfectionism and detail. We tend to lean in and obsessively try to fix. You think you need control to bring on a feeling of safety. Feeling anxious activates the fight-or-flight response, and you begin to panic; you leap into survival mode and become hypervigilant. When we lean in, we become overly controlling and make poor choices.

A very important tool to cope with anxiety is to "lean out." When you lean out, you engage in the energy of surrender. You send a message to the universe that you feel a bit of trust. You enter into an energy of allowing and not controlling. You send a message that you trust in life. The neural pathways of anxiety need to be interrupted by consistently stopping the thoughts that caused the panic. New neural pathways will be created the more the habitual anxiety thoughts are interrupted.

What Does Leaning Out Look Like?

Often dysfunctional relationships can cause people to lose their self-culture in a bid to save the relationship. One of my clients always felt dissatisfied with and was judgmental of her partner, who had clearly been doing his best in the face of having attention-deficit disorder (ADD), which made him unable to give her the kind of attention she felt she needed to feel safe in the relationship. She felt anxious about this. She would try to control him, berating him and pleading with him and feeling jealous of him and his activities. None of this got her what she desired, which was to feel that she was a priority in the relationship.

What she needed was simply to have her own life. She needed to lean out of him and lean back into herself. When I gave her this suggestion, a look of despair came over her face. She told me that nothing would ever change if she didn't take control of everything; in effect, be an overfunctioner. I asked her if what she had been doing was working for her. She said no. I told her to try something different. Even though this would cause immense fear, she was willing to give it a try. She started to discipline herself to not be as overly involved with her partner's comings and goings as she had been. She was leaning out. She began to find other activities to keep herself from the impulse to control her partner. She had been texting him five times a day, now she did not. She had been depending on him to drive her everywhere because she didn't know how to drive. She since learned how to drive. She took control of her own life and leaned out of his. The question was, would the relationship survive when her overfunctioning ceased to be the mainstay of the relationship?

What transpired was quite remarkable. Her partner began to seek her out more. He was now leaning into her because of the void that was created when she stopped leaning into him. Nature abhors a void; the void will be filled with something if you allow the void to be there in the first place. Anxiety will not permit the void, but interrupting the anxious thoughts will allow for a very healthy void to occur. Trust will occur, and new neural pathways will form.

Another example is when people are dealing with something they clearly have no control over, such as whether or not they will get the job they applied for, or if they will get the home they put an offer on. All these are serious causes for a departure from peaceful, trusting, authentic living, and anxiety takes over. These are all opportunities to lean out. A Zen proverb says "Let go or be dragged." The image is so clear; when there is too much trouble, the instinct is to hang on more, to lean in more. Do the opposite. Let go and decide to not be dragged. Lean out.

All of these strategies have the potential, if used regularly and diligently, to change your life. Remember, new neural pathways are the key, and to create them, repetition is required. Once the new pathways have been developed, the autoresponse to your triggers begins to shift. The process becomes easier over time.

Chapter Sixteen

THE POWER OF FORGIVENESS

> "To forgive is to set a prisoner free
> and discover that the prisoner was you."
> —LEWIS B. SMEDES, author of *Forgive and Forget: Healing the Hurts We Don't Deserve*

Pascale, who had been sexually abused repetitively by a family member during the early years of her childhood, was having a difficult time moving past the experience, even though she said she was now in a great marriage. She said she had every reason to be content, but she had lost the joy in her life. She sounded depressed and spoke of the constant resentment that kept bubbling up, the deep distrust she felt and the trouble she was having in letting go of the past. She said she used to be creative and enthusiastic, but had lost all that. She had trouble connecting with her husband, and anxiety was interrupting her ability to concentrate. She wanted to find her old self, but the past kept creeping into her consciousness, and she bemoaned not being able to get "her" back.

Pascale's family of origin had been in constant turmoil, which placed her in a very vulnerable position to begin with, and she had no one to protect her. Once a person suffers trauma and abuse, especially when there is no means of fighting or fleeing the situation, the trauma can become frozen in the person's nervous system. This can result in repetitive bouts of unexplained compulsive thinking, anxiety and depression. Through repetition, the system is looking to resolve and make sense of what was never resolved in the past. Even if the trauma was long ago, a person may relive the feelings and emotions over and over. These post-traumatic symptoms can also lie in remission for years, and then resurface later in life, destroying a person's quality of life.

One of the keys to resolving the trauma may have nothing to do with righting the wrongs of the past. In reality, we cannot go back in time and undo what was done. But we still can free ourselves.

Through therapy, Pascale learned that she had been choosing to hold onto the resentment. She realized that she was living as if she could change the past. She fantasized about retribution and some sort of justice that needed to come about. But it became increasingly obvious to her that her overfocusing on the past was destroying her present. I suggested that she might consider forgiveness. Not forgetting, but forgiving—a deep acceptance that the events of the past were truly over and could never be changed. She had to grieve and cry about this loss of hope that the past could be corrected. She had to feel compassion for herself and what she had been through. *She had to go through the mountain and emerge victorious on the other side*. And she did emerge! She was able to free herself of the depressive feelings that constantly overwhelmed her. She felt an inner freedom that was gained through the process of letting go of the hope that the past could change. She became focused on the present and the gratitude that she felt for it, as well as the gratitude she felt for surviving the past.

Viktor Frankl, one of the few who survived the horrors of the Auschwitz concentration camp in World War II, wrote in his seminal book *Man's Search for Meaning*, "When we are no longer able to change a situation … we are challenged to change ourselves."[1]

To move beyond surviving into thriving, you can choose to forgive; it is the freedom ticket back to peace and happiness.

Dr. Daniel Klassen, professor emeritus in education at Lakehead University in Thunder Bay, Ontario, author of *The Forgiveness Workbook* and founder of and counselor at The Listening Centre in Thunder Bay, is a leading expert on forgiveness. He says that there are proven benefits to forgiving, such as reduced anger, anxiety, depression and obsessive thoughts about the past, and an increase in self-esteem, optimism and hope.

When I introduce this idea to my clients, I often hear, "How can I forgive the horrors that someone has done to me?" I then redefine the concept of forgiveness, telling them that it is not about turning the other cheek or forgetting what happened. Instead, it is about freedom. In a presentation on forgiveness that I attended, Dr. Klassen said that to forgive is not to condone. If someone has been injured by another person, rather than seek retribution, which the offender deserves, the injured person has the right to *choose* to let go of any feeling of resentment, acknowledging that a wrong was done to him or her. As a result of this choice, the injured person cancels the offender's debt. This is a deep freedom from the events of the past.

Forgiveness has nothing to do with the other person. It is solely about the person who was hurt. When you go into forgiveness mode, you are taking back your life and your power. You are getting into the present moment versus losing yourself in the past or the other person.

---

1 Viktor E. Frankl, *Man's Search for Meaning: An Introduction to Logotherapy* (New York: Simon & Schuster, 1984), 116.

Even though revenge is something I have heard many talk about as something that they fanaticize about as giving them deep satisfaction, this is not what usually occurs. I heard a story a number of years ago on the radio about a woman who had lost her eyesight because her husband had doused her in acid. The man did go to jail, and he was sentenced to becoming blind. He was forced to undergo a procedure that blinded him. When the woman was interviewed, she clearly expressed that this did not make her feel better or as though she had been given retribution. Instead, she described how her levels of inner pain, guilt and anxiety increased because, even though this man had brutalized her, she did not wish her state of being on anyone, not even the man who had done this to her. She said that she did not feel free from the event at all.

Let us be clear, however, that forgiveness is definitely not about forgetting. That would be foolish. If you are going to continue the relationship with the offender, then new boundaries need to be established so that trust can be rebuilt. If that cannot happen, then the continuation of the relationship may not be possible. This is especially true if you are trying to overcome infidelity in a committed relationship.

You may choose to never see the offender again, even though you may have chosen to forgive him or her. Remember, forgiveness is not about the other person; it is about the injured party. Therefore, whatever is most healing for that person is what needs to be done.

The key here is that it is all about choice. Giving yourself the permission in the very beginning to withhold forgiveness may be where you need to start the forgiveness process. A feeling of empowerment needs to be brought forth into consciousness. As forgiveness is introduced, the energy of victimhood is slowly replaced with the energy of empowerment. To forgive is to choose to release, to choose to zero the debt and declare freedom.

From a spiritual perspective, forgiveness is forgiving the flawed soul that hurt you. And sometimes that is all a person can do. It is important to acknowledge that we are all flawed souls, traveling on our paths toward improvement. You may not be able to forgive the person who hurt you, but you can begin by forgiving the soul of that person. It is a place to start. When you can get in touch with this idea, you can begin the long journey of healing.

Another very important aspect to healing is forgiveness of oneself. So many people blame themselves for being in the situation that resulted in their being victimized. Self-forgiveness involves speaking gently to the child within; befriending the part that feels betrayed, invaded and shamed; and creating a nurturing relationship with that child so that peace can be made. A helpful exercise is to daily visualize yourself treating yourself as a gentle parent would, in a kind, generous and loving way. This will help build new neural pathways that go along with the new belief in self-love and self-forgiveness. This will help you to move beyond the traumas of the past.

For deep forgiveness, transcendence thinking is needed as well; that is, thinking in a way that enables you to transcend the event or the offence. This is a spiritual concept, in which you would ask questions such as, "What did I learn from those terrible events?" In this way, you can come to understand the lessons that may have been learned through the traumatic event. I find that people move so much faster into profound forgiveness and peace when they can begin to make sense of it all on a deeper, spiritual level. In reality, there is wisdom in the unfolding of a life, and even the most horrible situations are not here to merely torture us, but to teach us about ourselves and how strong we are. Meditation can serve as a tool to truly move us forward in this understanding.

Ultimately, forgiveness is a gift you give to yourself. The process of forgiveness is a rich one that provides great relief and great comfort. It is the way to truly realize your greatest potential. We were not meant to live in bitterness and resentment. We were meant to live with peace in our hearts.

Chapter Seventeen

WHAT IS YOUR RELATIONSHIP WITH MONEY?

Whenever I work with people who are carrying an unmanageable debt load and have issues around money, I observe that their emotional states are commensurate with their money problems, and the more debt they have, the lower their self-esteem seems to be. I always pose the question, "Which came first, the debt or the lack of self-esteem?" At first glance, you might think it is the debt and the money worry that cause the negative self-talk and low self-esteem; however, I believe the emotional issues come first, and they create the fertile soil for having a dysfunctional relationship with money.

Our money thoughts are influenced by what we have learned about money from parents, relatives, religious institutions, schools and others, and, if left unchecked, this way of thinking—our "money foundation"—will be with us forever. It is this foundation that guides all of our unconscious, subconscious and even conscious decisions about money matters, and it cannot change on its own. If you are not aware of your money foundation, then you cannot change it. We cannot change what we are not aware of.

T. Harv Ecker, a fantastic and inspiring speaker and author of *Secrets of the Millionaire Mind*, says, "It all comes down to this: if your subconscious 'financial blueprint' is not 'set' for success, nothing you learn, nothing you know, and nothing you do will make much of a difference." The only way to change your experience with money is to change your blueprint, which I feel is your "money foundation." You need to combat your poverty-thinking so that the money that does come in stays. That is, if you are someone who has a poverty mindset, even if you win the lottery, that money will not stay with you.

The various poverty beliefs, thoughts and actions that determine your money foundation determine your money vibration, and, as discussed in chapter one, your subconscious thoughts affect your vibration, which, in turn, affects what you attract to yourself. If the thoughts include feeling unworthy, feeling undeserving, feeling entitled to spend blindly, feeling obligated and being irresponsible, they will contribute to the loss of money and lack of prosperity in your life. It is a well-documented fact that many who win the lottery end up in a worse state financially after winning than prior to the win. They lose it all. They curse the lottery as the thing that ruined their lives. If only they had done some work on their money foundation!

The key to changing your money experience is to do a deep study of your life. Investigate your subconscious and conscious beliefs around money and wealth and write them all down. Look deeply at what you saw your parents and grandparents do with money. Were they constantly in debt? Did they keep a budget? Did they spend money without thought? Did they control you or others with money? Did they judge rich people as bad or crooked? Did they feel more at home with people who were struggling financially? Did they neglect talking to you about money because they thought to do so was rude? Did they ignore bills? Did they do their tax returns on time? Write down the answers to these questions and anything else you can think of that may have affected your beliefs around money. With these revelations, you can then change what is not supporting your "wealth foundation." You also need to see the true state of your finances, health and relationships. What is happening in one aspect of your life affects other areas too. If you are stingy with your love, chances are you are stingy with your money, and, similarly, if you are boundaryless with your emotions, you are probably boundaryless with your money. Look into the every aspect of your life if you want to see what is really going on in the money vibration realm.

A Change Is Coming

> "Thinking, learning, and acting can turn our genes on or off, thus shaping our brain anatomy and our behavior."
> —NORMAN DOIDGE, author of *The Brain That Changes Itself*

There is scientific evidence of the plasticity of the mind; that is, your mind is physically changeable if you give it what it needs to change. Imagination; visualization; focus; cognitive repetition; affirmations; meditation; and exposure to different thoughts, beliefs and life experiences are all ways to "plastify" your mind, or, in other words, change your mind into a new way of thinking and looking at things. Your mind will actually change physically in that new neural pathways will be created.

This is very exciting knowledge because even though changing your old and hardened beliefs around money will take effort and discipline on your part, it certainly can happen. There is no way around the work that needs to be done, but no matter your belief system about money, I want to assure you that change will happen if you put energy into it. If you focus on changing and bettering your money foundation, you will soon reap the rewards.

Tips to Change Your Money Foundation

1. Spend time every day visualizing yourself in a life where money is your friend as opposed to a source of difficulty. Be specific. The more you visualize yourself having a positive relationship with money with detailed imagery and specific visuals, the more you will begin to develop the neural pathways associated with the new beliefs.
2. Visualize yourself easily receiving money. I like to take my clients through a visualization in which they are standing in front of a bank machine and money begins to fall from the sky and float into their bank accounts. I ask them to visualize checks payable to them in high amounts and cash floating down into their hands, which they then deposit into the bank machine, and they are able to see the total amount in their accounts going up and up.
3. If guilt and low self-esteem are a problem for you, then work with a therapist to neutralize any of these destructive feelings. Work to forgive yourself on all levels. There is a wonderful mantra for prosperity called "Om Sri Maha Lakshmiyei Swaha" that I encourage you to repeat at least 108 times a day. Mantras help to change one's consciousness and, thus, one's vibration, and 108 is a sacred number based in ancient spiritual practices.

   The Om Sri Maha Lakshmiyei Swaha mantra, pronounced "om shree mah-ha laksh-mee-yei swah-ha," is a prayer to the Lakshmi deity. It is important to pronounce it as accurately as possible. Lakshmi brings material and spiritual wealth, prosperity and abundance. She is beautiful and is portrayed standing on a lotus blossom with her arms open and giving. I encourage you to visualize her gifting you with all the abundance the universe has to offer. Receive her gifts openly. Thomas Ashley-Farrand, who wrote the book *Healing Mantras*, says, "This mantra will greatly aid in the peaceful and harmonious transition to new and positive energy states."[1]

4. Track your spending for at least sixty days so you know exactly what you are doing with your money. Change your spending habits based on your new awareness. Keep all your receipts. Record all daily expenses and put them in different categories, such as mortgage or rent, household, groceries, meals out, auto and transit, personal care, clothing, travel and gifts. Record everything, including insurance, bank fees and what you put away as savings. A modern way to do this is to find an app for your smartphone that helps you to track your spending. This will help you get out of any denial you may be in about how you are spending your money.
5. Pay off debt diligently. See the clearing of your debt as a key pathway to creating a more harmonious relationship with money.
6. Seek out a support group that will assist you in staying on the journey. An organization that may help you is Debtors Anonymous. They have a 12-step program that addresses habitual and compulsive spending of money you do not have, causing you to incur unmanageable debt. Ideally, you could

1 Thomas Ashley-Farrand, *Healing Mantras: Using Sound Affirmations for Personal Power, Creativity, and Healing* (New York: Ballantine Books, 1999), 143.

take part in this program alongside therapy to deepen any changes and to share your experiences with people who are on similar journeys.

The path to shifting your vibration around money is a worthy one as we all deserve to have ease in life. As you go through the process of improving your relationship to money, you will find that your self-esteem and self-empowerment will increase by leaps and bounds. I encourage you to continually treat money with respect and to take personal responsibility for all of your decisions around money. You money foundation has the chance to transform into a positive and healthful experience for you. Know that you are worth it and you are valuable!

Chapter Eighteen

YOUR TWO VOICES WITHIN

As you make your way toward your self-culture, you are closer to hearing your own real voice as the loudest influence in your life. I believe that your self-culture voice is actually your soul's voice making its presence known to you. Eventually, with the work you do, it will be the loudest voice that you hear within yourself. I want to introduce you to the concept of the ego's voice versus the soul's voice. The ego is your personality and, at times, your lowest aspect, which is driven by fear, lack, distrust and insecurity. It is the brain delivering messages of oversafety, overprotection, self-judgment, criticism, fear and negativity.

This voice seems to be the brain sending seemingly logical messaging to be fearful of life. It actually normalizes fear. Do you have trouble coming out of negativity because your brain has convinced you that your negative thoughts are reasonable and truthful? Do you consistently indulge your chatterbox mind, never stopping long enough to allow an alternative thought to the fear and the self-doubt?

Your ego voice is not just your brain; it is the worry center of your brain that is fed by the daily news, the messages of the fear-mongers and memories of a traumatic childhood. At every turn, your brain looks to normalize the fear and tells you that it is right for you to doubt life and yourself. It gives you all kinds of logical reasons why you should not risk trying new things. It tells you to be afraid of intimacy because it is scary and risky. It tells you to stay safe at all costs and to live within your comfort zone forever. It threatens your ability to grow, be adventurous and speak up for yourself.

You do not need to be the victim of your seemingly logical brain/ego voice. You, the real you, are not your brain or your thoughts. You have another voice within you—your soul voice. Your self-culture! This voice is just as clear if you allow it to emerge. It is the expression of love and joy and all that you truly are. It is ready for you to finally listen; you just need to tap into it. You may not be used to hearing this voice, but I promise you, we all have it. You just need to give it space and permission to come out. It is waiting for you to allow it to show itself.

Which Inner Voice Are You Feeding?

Through awareness, you will know which voice you are giving power to.

The Ego/Personality/Brain Voice

- Your ego voice is likely the one you are most familiar with and use all the time.
- It is usually full of fear and self-doubt.
- It is the part of you that is drowning in "duality judgment": "This is good; that is bad." This is where most of your suffering emerges from. When we judge things as good or bad, our judgmentalism prevents us from learning from the events.
- The ego is constantly in comparison mode. "The grass is always greener over there," it says. There is a deep fear of missing out on something that seems better elsewhere.
- It drowns you in criticism of self and others.

- It is the part of you that is obsessed with the past and the future. You are not in the present moment when in the ego voice.
- Gratitude is lost when the ego is in charge.
- It is the worrier part of you that is enslaved by dread.
- There is nothing free or light when you are in this voice; instead, there is heaviness in your life when it is active.
- When you feed this voice, you are usually being influenced by other people's expectations, judgments and perspectives.
- It usually represents your hurt child, who is having a field day, ruining your day and your life with terrible decisions.
- If left to its own devices, the ego/personality/brain voice will run amuck and do its best to destroy your life.

The Soul Voice

- When your soul voice is speaking, judgment stops and acceptance of what is in front of you emerges.
- It is not reactive; it is accepting.
- You are less duality-oriented: "This just is what it is."
- The soul voice accepts life with equanimity; for example, when the soul voice is active, you are saying, "This is interesting. What can I learn here?" about all that you encounter. Your inner commentary on life is more neutral and detached. You experience the depth of experiences, but you do not attach judgment to the experiences. The judgment is what sends a person into a rabbit hole of self-annihilation.
- You know you are in your soul voice when you are in the present day versus obsessing about the past and or the future.
- You know you are in your soul voice when you are more adult and feel full and less needy or like a victim.

- The soul voice encourages self-love, self-empowerment and self-acceptance.
- The soul voice encourages trust and faith versus fear and resentment.
- You are more freedom-oriented.
- You are able to take more risks and try new things because fright and panic are not hammering down on you.
- You are not enslaved by other people's expectations.
- You are more trusting and loving.

It is your choice to feed one voice or the other, but, clearly, the soul voice is a recipe for a more joyful life and a clear pathway toward self-culture. There is an old story that speaks of two hungry lions circling a village. One lion is called "fear" and the other is called "love." The villagers, being nonviolent in nature, want to allow both to live, but they have only enough food for one to survive. The children ask the elders which lion is going to survive. The elders respond, "The one you feed." This is no different from your two voices within. The voice you feed the most with your attention is the one that will survive and eventually take over your life. You can decide at any given moment to be judgmental or to be accepting; to be past- or future-oriented or to be fully in the present moment; to be in your hurt child, making reckless decisions, or your adult self, relishing the magnificence of life. Choose your soul voice often and see your life's purpose unfold effortlessly. Choose your soul voice and find your self-culture.

Chapter Nineteen

BREAKING THE CYCLE OF DYSFUNCTION

Final Lessons

The Darkness within Has Wisdom to Offer You

Connie came to see me, complaining bitterly about the dysfunctional behavior among her group of friends, with whom she'd been friends since high school. One particular person in this group was a charming, effusive individual, but he had a nasty, embittered, judgmental side to him. Connie was frequently the object of his judgment and cold-shoulder treatment, making her feel as though she were on a roller-coaster ride, and she didn't understand why she was constantly looking for his approval.

Connie was an intelligent person, but she was suffering and feeling belittled by his behavior toward her. She was in a dark place, which elicited a dysfunctional need in her for approval from someone she didn't even like very much. She didn't understand this, so she judged him and complained about him, saying, "He's a jerk" and "He's no good." Through therapy, she finally began to understand that all her complaining about him was her codependence, which was stopping her from looking within and analyzing her own dark side in this situation. Her preoccupation with looking outside herself for answers was preventing her from looking within and becoming conscious of this darkness that was lying in the murky waters of her unconscious. Even though she was tempted to avoid this inner, painful exploration, it was from within this darkness that she would learn and grow.

Once she moved from him and into herself, she was able to open up the murky waters and started shining a light on the darkness. The unconscious, unaware part of her began to make its presence known and inform her about what was operating within her. This process led her to understand that she was seeking approval from someone outside herself due to her unresolved family-culture issues. She learned that though she thought she had a handle on her lack of self-esteem and deep insecurities, she clearly had some work to do. She had not been aware because she had constantly been looking outside herself as a habit. She kept saying he was wrong or they were wrong, never looking within. As a result, she had overlooked the nuggets of gold that existed had she looked within herself and asked, "What is this dark part of me trying to tell me?"

Connie's growth, development and evolution toward her true self-culture occurred when she stopped looking at him and began to look at the dark side within herself. She stopped asking "Why is he doing this to me?" and started asking the right questions: "Who am I really?" "What am I doing here?" and "Why do I keep repeating this feeling?"

I invite you to embrace the darkness within yourself because the opportunity for growth and learning lies within that darkness.

Get Out of Your Comfort Zone: Change Is Needed!

Many people try to avoid change to avoid anxiety and stress; yet profound unhappiness can ensue if you are paralyzed and remain stagnant. Going after your life purpose, and thus your self-culture, inevitably involves change. I often see people in my office who are deeply dissatisfied with their lives because they have not changed what needed to change in their lives, and as a result, they stagnated by staying in relationships that were no longer healthy, jobs that were not satisfying or situations that were not good for them. They employed the ego/brain logic that is led by fear and said, "I would rather stay in this dissatisfying, negative, emotionally draining situation than risk change." "Better stick with what is familiar and comfortable rather than risk going into the unknown." But deep unhappiness that turns into depression tends to beckon a fundamental need for change!

We know that dissatisfaction is the mother of change. But if you numb yourself to the feelings of dissatisfaction by constantly distracting yourself, engaging in addiction and living in denial about what you truly feel, you will stay in situations that are deeply wrong for you and, as a result, you will not be happy with your life.

To facilitate change in a way that is less scary, employ the spiritual principle of being in the present moment. This combats toxic future-worrying. It is okay to future-plan, but not to future-worry! It keeps you from doing what your soul craves. Put one foot in front of the other. Track your thoughts and don't let them get out of control by challenging the irrational "fear-thoughts." Allow yourself to make a small change at a time; hold it, assess it, and then continue to make the next change; hold this change, and then assess it, and you'll find you get to the other side in a healthy and emotionally together way. If you change in this clear, calm and present-moment–oriented way, you will be more likely to succeed without undue stress. I also recommend affirmations, positive visualizations, meditation and deep breathing so that you can remain relaxed as you delve into the unknown on the journey toward your life purpose and into your self-culture.

The Buck Stops Here!

Multigenerational dysfunction is pervasive. People do to their kids what was done to them largely because they are unaware and mired in their own rage and shame. Not recognizing this results in the dysfunction continuing through the generations, and with each generation, the abuse becomes more ingrained and more destructive.

Recently I witnessed the result of multigenerations of dysfunction, all stemming from the deep-rooted hurt and resentment of a mother, five generations back, who was overly involved with her son and very neglectful of her daughter. That daughter then had two children, and she did the same thing, unconsciously pampering her son and neglecting her daughter. That daughter had two kids, and she perpetrated the rage on her children, yelling and screaming bloody hell at them. Her deep anger, resentment and frustrations were launched on her children, and then on to the next generation, so the dynamic continued with the woman who finally came in to see me. My heart went out to her because, as an adult, she felt deeply sad, hurt, harmed, shocked and traumatized by the emotional abuse she had endured due to her mother's frustration and rage attacks. It is human nature not to want to behave this way, and yet this woman was behaving in the same way with her child. It's tragic to see such repetition occur, often without awareness by the perpetrator, and nothing will change without the person's being conscious of the pattern.

If you are caught up in such a family pattern, you need to declare to yourself that the buck stops with you—that the dysfunction stops with you! You need to choose to stop the pattern and family dynamic immediately. You must bring forward an awareness of your behavior as soon as you realize you are lashing out at your children, and then get into some therapy so you can process this shame that you are carrying and perpetrating into the next generation. Awareness and therapy are required for there to be change.

Without awareness and consciousness, the pattern gets worse and more ingrained with each generation. But you can stop it. I encourage you to look deeply into your soul and see whether you are repeating a family dynamic, and if you are, take responsibility for what you are doing, which clearly is no longer your mother's fault, your father's fault or your grandmother's fault. It is not your fault either, but it is your responsibility! It's yours, and you have to decide not to do this to your life or to the next generation. For multigenerational dysfunction to stop, you need to empower yourself, value yourself, know yourself and advocate for yourself. You need to step into your self-culture.

Following is a list of "rights" that I invite you to say often and embrace:

1. I have the right to be my authentic self.
2. I have the right to have and experience my feelings.
3. I have the right to feel anger and to express it in responsible and constructive ways.
4. I have the right to say no, without explaining or feeling guilty, when I feel something is not right or I feel unsafe.
5. I have the right to not feel bad or guilty just because another person does not like me or what I do, say, think or feel.
6. I have the right to have boundaries and to set limits in a fair and kind way.
7. I have the right to stick to my values and to honor my integrity.

8. I have the right to speak up when I think others are manipulating me or treating me unfairly.
9. I have the right to change my mind.
10. I have the right to be imperfect.
11. I have the right to make mistakes, to be unsure and to say "I don't know" without feeling guilty, dumb or stupid.
12. I have the right to not be affected by the opinions, tone or behavior of others.
13. I have the right to take full responsibility for my life.
14. I have the right to be joyful, healthy and confident.
15. I have the right to embrace and live my self-culture, even though it may be different from my family culture.

Now that you have read this book, I highly recommend that you go back over the exercises and incorporate them into your daily practice. Remember, your thoughts affect the neural pathways in your brain. These thoughts help to establish your vibration, which, in turn, affects what you attract to yourself. Thus, new thoughts change your vibration and what you attract to yourself. You create new thoughts by exposing yourself to new environments, people, reading, visualizations and actions, and by regularly repeating them all in many different ways. The new normal that you create will solidify if you practice, practice, practice. Eventually, that new normal will simply be your normal life.

As you make your way toward your self-culture, you will begin to feel a "rightness" deep within the core of your whole being. The transformations you experience on all levels will be amazing. I am honored to be a witness to such transformations daily. I have so much respect and admiration for all who choose to go on this journey of selfhood. So many of the people I have worked with are passionately living their self-culture, and I am humbled by the permission they have given me to walk alongside them as they climbed out of the rabbit hole and began their expedition. Each and every one who managed to climb out of the life they were unhappy with had to have persistence, perseverance, diligence and focus as they went through this sometimes lonely journey.

You will need to grieve for what you leave behind. You may have self-doubt. You will most probably feel lost initially. But remember, for every feeling of loss, loneliness or emptiness, there will be a new normal that you specifically designed for yourself to live in. No one else has the privilege of designing your life other than yourself. Also, know that the more you endeavor to make yourself happy, joyful and authentic, the more the planet will benefit. Finding your self-culture ultimately means that you will be able to benefit the people around the planet and the universe as a whole. It is my opinion that when you live your self-culture fully, you carry a great responsibility with you to share what you know with others and to use the joy you experience to improve the world at large. May you find, keep and become your self-culture!

Appendix I

DEEP RELAXATION EXERCISE

For this exercise, you need to know where your *pisiform bone* is. Derived from the Latin word *pisum*, which means "pea," this is a pea-size, knobbly wrist bone. If you look at one of your hands with your palm facing up, this bone is located where the inner bone of your forearm meets your wrist. When you massage around this bone (of either hand), you will experience an almost immediate feeling of relaxation.

In Traditional Chinese Medicine (TCM), the area of the pisiform bone is an acupuncture point (the HT 7) along the heart meridian that helps to calm anxiety, ease an overactive mind and relieve insomnia.[1]

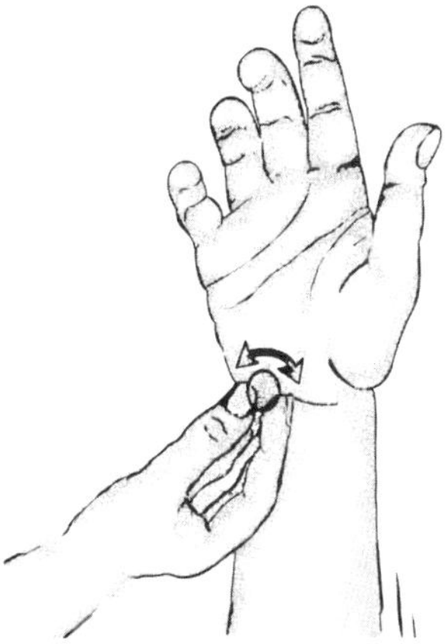

Pisiform Bone

1 Yin Yang House, "HT 7 Acupuncture Point – Shen Men – Heart Meridian" (2013), www.yinyanghouse.com/acupuncturepoints/ht7.

Begin by putting on some gentle, soothing instrumental music. This unobtrusive sound will help to calm your mind, emotions and body as you begin the exercise. You may also wish to disperse a relaxing aromatherapy oil into the room.

Next, get into a comfortable position, either sitting or lying, and then close your eyes and begin to breathe slowly. Then, with one hand, find the pisiform bone on the other hand and begin to massage all around it. As you massage it, you will feel yourself slowing down and feeling relaxed. Continue to do this and notice if there is a point that feels tight or tense. After a few minutes, hold this point gently, and as you continue to breathe, mentally send your breath to that spot.

Tip: Try working on your pisiform bone while in a traffic jam!

Still applying gentle pressure to the tissue around and on your pisiform bone, continue to breathe slowly, and then bring your awareness to your body. Starting with your feet, slowly move your attention up through your entire body—calves, knees, thighs, hips, and all the way up to your face and head. Before you move from one area to another, ask yourself "What do I feel here?" and make mental notes of what comes up.

Once you have scanned your body in this way, pick an area where you felt the most pain and, keeping your eyes closed, slowly bring your attention to the pain.

Intend to stay on the edge of the pain initially rather than jumping immediately to the center of it.

As you focus on the pain, begin an inner dialogue with it. Ask the pain to communicate with you in any way it can. Invite any insights to gently emerge as a word, a memory, a phrase, an image or just a vague idea, rather than have them impose themselves on you. It is important not to rush; the slower the better. Don't get frustrated if nothing comes at first. Be patient, kind and compassionate with yourself. When in doubt *breathe slowly*. Take your time and allow space for awareness to come forth.

Once insights to the root of your pain emerge, try to visualize the stronger part of yourself alongside the part of you that is not as stable. As in the case study with Jane in chapter two, if you discover a hurt child within yourself, you can call upon your more balanced adult self to comfort the hurt child. Stay with this image and feeling for a while.

After you have connected with the source of your pain, begin to visualize yourself in your real life taking charge of a situation in which you may have previously felt powerless. Try to make this image as realistic as possible. Invite yourself to feel empowered, strong and in charge of the situation. *Breathe slowly* as you do this, and once you have a strong image, visualize yourself placing it in and anchoring it to your heart area. This will then be your anchor that you can call upon when you need it. (Continue to apply gentle pressure to your pisiform bone throughout the exercise; the relaxation it brings you will be beneficial to you as you remember past events.)

To end the exercise, bring your awareness back to your breathing and slowly open your eyes and allow yourself come back to the room. Take time to stretch before you slowly stand up and move around again.

Norman Doidge, MD, psychiatrist, researcher and author of *The Brain That Changes Itself: Stories of Personal Triumph from the Frontiers of Brain Science*, says that using one's imagination to visualize a change stimulates the brain to reorganize and create new neural pathways associated with the new thoughts, feelings and ways of being. Thus, the new normal becomes easier to maintain.

Once you have completed this exercise, take pen to paper and journal what you became aware of and what you felt. Try to be as specific as possible. You can also use colored pencils to make multicolored drawings of the images you visualized. The more senses you engage, the more new neural pathways you will create. See it, feel it, visualize it, write it, say it, hear it, draw it!

Appendix II

REPARENTING YOURSELF

The only real way to move beyond the scars of your upbringing and the anger you may have for your parents is to reparent yourself. You need to make yourself a priority and treat yourself as you wish you had been treated as a child. You need to learn to be kind, loving, compassionate and forgiving toward yourself. With daily repetition and the resulting laying down of new neural pathways, this exercise will allow you to heal the wounds of the past. Only then will you be able to move into a real adulthood, in which you need very little from your parents, and change what is wrong in your life.

To begin the exercise, sit quietly in a room by yourself. Visualize yourself as a child. Pick an age (preferably under the age of eight) that is significant to you, such as the first time you felt alone, or the first time you realized that not everything in life would go smoothly. Imagine yourself taking care of yourself as a little child. See yourself giving this child within your unconditional, nurturing love. See yourself being the parent you needed and didn't have. Imagine yourself as the calm and patient parent taking part in activities with the child; for example, gently brushing the child's hair, building a sand castle together, pushing the happy child on a swing or riding a merry-go-round together and laughing. Say to yourself as a child, "You are enough. You matter. You are important to me. You are talented and beautiful, and I love you. I will always love you. You can count on me now." And then affirm to yourself often: "I am enough. I have enough. There is more than enough in the universe for me." These affirmations will go to your core; they work to fill feelings of emptiness and loneliness that may happen initially as you individuate. I recommend you repeat these affirmations and do this exercise every night before you fall asleep.

If you do this, you will begin to make choices that demonstrate that you consider yourself to be a valuable person. You will be discerning about the people you allow into your life and the choices you make. You will show the child within that you can be trusted to be a loving and responsible parent to yourself. In time, you will have retrained your whole being to be self-loving and self-nurturing.

Appendix III

EXERCISE FOR DEVELOPING YOUR SELF-CULTURE

Get a pen and paper and sit quietly in a comfortable chair at a desk or other writing surface. Close your eyes and begin to breathe slowly and continuously without pauses, so that as soon as you get to the top of the inhale, begin to exhale, and when you get to the bottom of the exhale, begin to inhale. Repeat this pattern five times, and then open your eyes and ask yourself the following questions, taking your time to answer each one. Allow your inner voice to come up and be honest and nonjudgmental with yourself as you write down your answers.

1. What "part" of myself am I not living?
2. What do I long to express, explore and bring to light at this moment?
3. What in my self-culture do I need to unearth?

As you answer these questions, you will begin to see the real you coming to life on the page. Now you can work with what you have written to explore even further. Read over your answers and try to come up with two or three sentences that describe what you have expressed. Begin each sentence with "I" and write clearly and concisely in the present tense. These sentences will be your personal statements that open the door to your self-culture. For example, someone might write the following:

1. I draw clear boundaries in my life, especially with my family and friends.
2. I feel empowered to say no whenever I need to.
3. I make myself a priority at all times.

You can then use each of these three statements as mission statements, which you can use in the exercise in appendix IV, "Exercise for Anchoring New Neural Pathways."

Appendix IV

EXERCISE FOR ANCHORING NEW NEURAL PATHWAYS

This wonderful exercise is a way to anchor your new beliefs into your deeper consciousness and the core of your being. It is a multilayered method that is done by using three techniques at the same time: visual, auditory and kinesthetic. Don't worry if you don't believe what you are saying, visualizing or doing; just "fake it until you make it!"[1]

1. **Your visual anchor:** Visualize yourself in a real-life scene living your self-culture.
2. **Your auditory anchor:** Say out loud one of your mission statements that you created in the exercise in appendix III, "Exercise for Developing Your Self-Culture."
3. **Your kinesthetic anchor:** While you say your statement and visualize your scene, make a movement; for example, put your hand to your heart, interlace your fingers or do the "cross crawl," in which you put your right elbow on your left knee and then your left elbow on your right knee, and then repeat the sequence for about twenty seconds.

---

1 "Fake it until you make it" derives from the neuro-linguistic programming (NLP) principle that it isn't necessary to understand the hows and whys of what you are doing, but by the Law of Cause and Effect, where like causes produce like effects, by acting a part, you can make it a reality.

When you do all three at the same time, you drive your new beliefs deeper into your consciousness, which makes the new neural pathways thicker and, therefore, your new behavior patterns easier to maintain.

You can do this exercise in a private or a public setting. It is an especially important exercise to do if you are in the middle of a situation that triggers an old behavior pattern. If you are in a public situation, as soon as you notice an old reaction coming to the surface, I recommend that you begin to privately call on your visual anchor and discreetly do your kinesthetic anchor. The verbal anchor may be more difficult to do quietly; however, this is okay, especially if you have worked with all three anchors previously and repetitively in private. The more you practice these exercises on your own, the further you will be on your way to creating new neural pathways.

Appendix V

VISUALIZATION TO TRANSFORM YOUR INNER BULLY INTO A SUPPORTIVE COACH

Sit in a calm space and close your eyes. Imagine yourself in a peaceful, natural setting. Call forth the bully in you; for example, you could imagine in detail a schoolyard bully. In your mind's eye, invite the bully to sit down with you. Be prepared to be open and nonjudgmental as you begin to ask the bully the following key questions and wait patiently for the responses:

1. What are you trying to do for me?
2. What is your positive purpose in my life?
3. What do you seek to accomplish by constantly being in my life?

The more open you are, the more information you will gather, and the more likely you will be able to neutralize and, ultimately, transform your destructive inner bully. If you listen carefully, the bully will tell you that it is trying to make you a better person. It is trying to protect you from failure and disappointment. It is trying to encourage you to be the best you can be. However, as you know, it is failing miserably at this task because of its attitude and abusive tone.

Once you have heard the answers to your questions, you can tell the bully that you understand what it is trying to do for you.

Tell the bully that its method is not effective. Thank the bully for its efforts, but that a new way is needed now.

It is important that you understand that this is a process of befriending your darker side; that is, integrating it into your whole being so that it knows that you are finally listening carefully to its underlying positive message, and that it will not have to yell as loudly at you to be heard. This is the way to transform the bully within yourself.

Continue to slowly visualize the bully becoming a more aligned version of itself—a supportive and encouraging coach. Imagine this inner coach in detail, allowing its gentle, encouraging—yet strong—voice to emerge. Your coach might say to you, "You are precious and lovable, and you deserve gentleness as you ease into your transitions," "I believe in you," "Bit by bit you are getting to your goal" and "Consistency is the key to your success. Stick with it. I know you can do it."

The coach within you will encourage you to try the 80/20 rule: 80% of the time, move in your desired new direction, such as standing up for yourself, being authentic, eating well, spending wisely or exercising, but do it gently, lovingly and kindly! Don't be too punishing! For the other 20% of the time, you may slip back to your old ways, but all the while you know that you are slowly improving. Tell yourself that every day you are getting better and better. Remember, slow change is permanent change. Be kind to yourself. Remember that your inner child needs gentle dialogue so it can get on board and stop sabotaging the adult who's trying to make positive life changes.

Appendix VI

SELF-COMFORTING HUGGING EXERCISE

This exercise is an opportunity for you to spend time acknowledging your feelings in a loving and supportive way, even if no one else has. It is part of the process of becoming mentally and emotionally fit as described in chapter nine, "Getting in 'Right' Relationship with Self and Life." Use it to ease the discomfort of moving out of your comfort zone as you seek your own self-culture, and to relax any anxiety, self-doubt and nervous feelings you might have.

The multilayered approach in this exercise, whereby you physically hug yourself, whisper supportive words and visualize kind parental energy, will encourage new neural pathways to develop much faster, which, in turn, will make it easier for you to be kind and loving toward yourself. The positive feelings you gain will envelop your very energy center.

You will feel absolutely amazing every time you engage in this self-comforting exercise. Take five to ten minutes during your day to do it, and do it often—make it a habit.

Find a quiet place with no distractions, sit or lie down comfortably, close your eyes and breathe deeply. Fold your arms around yourself in a hugging embrace and begin to whisper soft, loving and encouraging words to yourself, such as "It's going to be alright," "Shuuush, you are safe," "I love you," "I understand you," "I hear you," "You are great, and know I am always here for you," "I have compassion for you" and "You are not alone." Try to rock yourself a little as you would a fearful child who needs comforting. Be like a kind, supportive parent. With your eyes still closed, visualize the scene to drive the experience deep into your consciousness. Really connect with all your thoughts and feelings of comfort and love. Hold onto your feelings, and then slowly open your eyes and stretch before standing up and getting on with your day.

Appendix VII

DIALOGUE WITH SELF WHILE EATING EXERCISE

When you eat, make sure you are in a peaceful state. Set a lovely table for yourself. Create an atmosphere of calm.

Slowly, before you put any food in your mouth, begin to dialogue with your body; let it know that food is coming and ask it to prepare itself.

Wait—allow your body to respond. You need to be attuned to your body's subtle messaging so that you know that it is calm and ready to accept the food. Then you can begin to eat.

Chew your food slowly and well and wait a moment between bites. Your body needs time to register what it is being given; it needs time to send messages to your brain so that the food will be processed with the appropriate digestive enzymes. Also, when you eat slowly, you will more accurately register when you have had enough food as it takes at least fifteen minutes after you finish eating before you get the message that you are full. When you eat slowly, the more aware you will be of your body's messages and the more appropriately you will respond to them.

Once you have finished eating, take time to dialogue with any emotions that may come up at that time.

There is no set outcome for this exercise, but it gives you the opportunity to eat consciously so that you create more harmony and balance in your body. You will learn to understand what your body needs when you have cravings, rather than turning to quick fixes. Your body will be grateful that you are finally listening to it, and it will reward you with less intensive messages in the form of uncomfortable symptoms.

Appendix VIII

GROUNDING EXERCISE

This exercise slows you down so that you can feel a connection with yourself.

Sit in a chair or lie down comfortably on your back and close your eyes. Inhale and exhale deeply and slowly and feel yourself relax.

When you are relaxed, visualize yourself as a tree—a very large oak tree. Stay with this image until you are one with the oak tree. Feel that your spine is surrounded by this strong, solid oak trunk, transferring power to your spine .

Continue to breathe slowly and deeply, and as you exhale, feel your breath go down your spine to your legs and feet and into the ground, and imagine roots growing out of your feet. Imagine with each exhale that your breath is growing the roots deep into the center of Mother Earth.

After many slow breaths, the roots to your oak tree grow deeper and deeper into the ground, where you finally encounter a large metal anchor. Take the time to smell and feel the earth, and then imagine your breath directing the roots to wrap themselves around the anchor. Spend time visualizing and feeling this deep connection of your roots to this anchor. Imagine yourself tugging at the roots and feeling how connected they are to the anchor.

Relax and enjoy the feeling of strength and groundedness, and then slowly bring yourself back to the surface, open your eyes, stretch and enjoy the feeling before standing up again.

Every time you feel flighty or disconnected from yourself, it is a sign that you need to ground yourself. Do this visualization often. Eventually all you will need to do is say "ground!" or "oak tree!" to yourself, and the feeling of groundedness will come over you. From this perspective, you will be able to be more in touch with your deeper self.

Appendix IX

SUBMARINE EXERCISE

When you feel anxious, your body may respond by tightening, even though you have no idea as to what caused your anxiety. At these times, stop, sit down and close your eyes. Imagine a tiny submarine entering your body and you are in the submarine. Use your imagination to direct the submarine to the tight and tense place in your body and hover there. You are the captain, and you are driving the submarine. You have the ability to communicate with your body just by sending it your thoughts. Notice that as you do this, you begin to calm down. Give yourself the space to ask the tense part of your body, "What is this tension all about?" Pause and wait for the answers to emerge. Very soon you will have information that is buried there. A fear, fleeting worry or passing paranoia about something that may have been vague or you were too busy to cognitively process often shows up.

This exercise gives you a chance to hear what your anxiety is all about, instead of its being just a heap of feelings that are all mixed up and overwhelming. As soon as the answer comes, you will feel a sense of relief and a loosening of the tension. You can then dialogue with this tightness. For example, you can feed yourself positive and logical information such as "I hear you are worried about what that person is thinking about you, but, in truth, what other people think is not my business," or "I hear you are obsessing about what happened before, but the past is over. We are in the present moment now, and all is well and safe."

When you slow down your cognitive brain, you are more able to be reasonable and rational about what triggered your anxiety. This is an opportunity for your mind to become disciplined by your intention. If your intention is to calm yourself down, then this is a great way to effortlessly begin going in that direction.

Appendix X

WHITE-LIGHT EXERCISE

A good way to create calmness within yourself, especially when you are in a new environment or you are stepping into a situation that is familiar but anxiety-provoking, is to imagine that a dome of white protective light is surrounding you. Take a moment to visualize the creation of a wonderfully safe dome that you place around yourself. Once in the dome, allow your mind to focus on a feeling of ease as you make contact with other people. This may give you a sense that you can be in contact with others without feeling invaded by what you perceive they may be thinking or doing. Anxiety can make a person overly sensitive to others, and this visualization assists in mitigating the need to be overly reactive to other people. Practice taking the dome with you as you navigate the different events of your life.

I also suggest visualizing yourself putting a white light over other people. Take the time to visualize a person you care about being protected by this dome of white light. For example, an anxious parent can visualize himself or herself putting a white light over their child as the child walks to school, or as the child enters the car-pool vehicle, or a friend may visualize himself or herself putting a white light over a friend who is undergoing an operation. This act of sending the energy of protection to watch over those you care about may calm the anxiety that is triggered by your worry over others.

SELECTED BIBLIOGRAPHY

This bibliography is by no means a complete record of all the sources I consulted in the making of this book. Rather, it indicates the range of reading that formed my ideas, and it serves as a list of works that I recommend if you wish to pursue the teachings in this book in more detail.

Ashley-Farrand, Thomas. *Healing Mantras: Using Sound Affirmations for Personal Power, Creativity, and Healing*. New York: Ballantine Books, 1999.

Beattie, Melody. *Codependent No More: How to Stop Controlling Others and Start Caring for Yourself*. Center City, MN: Hazelden Foundation, 1992.

Carter, Steven, and Julia Sokol. *He's Scared, She's Scared: Understanding the Hidden Fears That Sabotage Your Relationships*. New York: Dell Publishing, 1993.

Doidge, Norman. *The Brain That Changes Itself: Stories of Personal Triumph from the Frontiers of Brain Science*. London: Penguin Books, 2007.

Dyer, Wayne W. *Your Sacred Self: Making the Decision to Be Free*. New York: HarperCollins, 1995.

Eker, T. Harv. *Secrets of the Millionaire Mind: Mastering the Inner Game of Wealth*. New York: HarperCollins, 2005.

Frankl, Viktor E. *Man's Search for Meaning: An Introduction to Logotherapy*. New York: Simon & Schuster, 1984.

Hay, Louise. *The Power Is within You*. Carlsbad, CA: Hay House Inc., 1991.

———. *You Can Heal Your Life*. Carlsbad, CA: Hay House Inc., 1999.

Katie, Byron, and Stephen Mitchell. *Loving What Is: Four Questions That Can Change Your Life*. New York: Three Rivers Press, 2002.

Klassen, Daniel. *The Forgiveness Workbook*. Thunder Bay, ON: Daniel Klassen, 2003

Lerner, Harriet Goldhor. *The Dance of Anger; A Woman's Guide to Changing the Patterns of Intimate Relationships*. New York: Harper & Row, 1985.

———. *The Dance of Intimacy: A Woman's Guide to Courageous Acts of Change in Key Relationships*. New York: Harper & Row, 1989.

Levine, Peter A. *Waking the Tiger; Healing Trauma*. Berkeley, CA: North Atlantic Books, 1997.

Smedes, Lewis B. *Forgive and Forget: Healing the Hurts We Don't Deserve*. San Francisco: HarperCollins, 1996.

Tolle, Eckhart. *The Power of Now: A Guide to Spiritual Enlightenment*. Novato, CA: New World Library, 2004.

Tylor, Edward Burnett. *Primitive Culture: Researches into the Development of Mythology, Philosophy, Religion, Art, and Custom*, Vol. 1. London: John Murray, 1871.

Williamson, Marianne. *A Return to Love: Reflections on the Principles of "A Course in Miracles."* New York: HarperCollins, 1992.

ABOUT THE AUTHOR

Victoria Lorient-Faibish is nothing if not eclectic. Born in Montreal and having grown up in Rio de Janeiro, Brazil, and Lisbon, Portugal, to a Portuguese Catholic mother and a Romanian Jewish father, Victoria today finds her home in Toronto, Canada, with her beloved husband of twenty-two years. Her influences include Buddhism, shamanism, osteopathy, physical fitness, music, theater, visualization and meditation, as well as modern and traditional psychotherapy.

In 1990, after the death of her father, Victoria returned from living in Cozumel, Mexico, where she was exposed to the subtle yet magnetic energy of the Mayan Indians. There she was exposed to hands-on energy work. Her return to Toronto set her on a journey of spiritual and emotional self-discovery that included a stint in the theater, where she wrote, starred in and produced a number of soul-exploring plays, including the critically acclaimed play *Coming Out of the Fridge*, a serious comedy about eating disorders and body consciousness. At the same time, she studied a plethora of holistic body-centered modalities, including reflexology, therapeutic touch, craniosacral therapy, reiki and her beloved and phenomenal polarity therapy. This mélange became the foundation of her busy private holistic practice in Toronto, which beckoned the need for a master's degree in educational psychology as her practice began to evolve past the body and into the realms of emotional transformation. This became the basis for her brand of holistic psychotherapy, which works with the mind, body and soul to effect monumental change in her clients' lives.

This book is a work of passion that began in 2007, when she started recording videos on YouTube about various topics that were delved into at the office. The public's response has been incredible as the hunger to find one's self-culture continues to be a key for people who are on a quest for self-love and happiness. The transcribed videos became the foundation for the chapters in this book.

Today, Victoria is thrilled to bring the work she does in her office to the world at large, where people can use the case studies, teachings and exercises in this book as they go on the path toward finding their self-culture.

For more information, please visit www.visualizationworks.com and www.self-culture.com.

INDEX

Information in footnotes is indicated by page and note number; for example, 1n2.

D

E